Discovering Music in Early Childhood

DISCOVERING MUSIC IN EARLY CHILDHOOD

SALLY MOOMAW
University of Cincinnati

Allyn and Bacon, Inc.
Boston   London   Sydney   Toronto

Series Editor: Jeffery W. Johnston

Library of Congress Cataloging in Publication Data

Moomaw, Sally, 1948–
    Discovering music in early childhood.

    Bibliography: p.
    Includes index.
    1. Nursery schools—Music.   2. Kindergarten—Music.
3. School music—Instruction and study.   I. Title.
MTl.M818   1984   372.8'7   83-15392
ISBN 0-205-08083-9

Printed in the United States of America
10 9 8 7 6 5 4 3 2 1 88 87 86 85 84

Contents

v

Preface

ANYONE WHO lives or works with young children soon discovers that they love music. They sing spontaneously as they play. They clap their hands and move their bodies to the sounds they hear, and they experiment over and over with creating sound. Music, sound, and movement are intrinsic to the learning experiences of young children. It seems unfortunate, then, that many preschool and primary teachers do not include music experiences in their curriculum, and that others do only a few familiar finger plays. Many adults feel inadequate in the area of music. They believe that they need years of training or experience with instruments to know enough about music to explore music with young children.

Any teacher can plan and carry out music activities with children just as he or she can do art without being an artist, science without being a scientist, and large-muscle work without being a gymnast. This book is designed to assist non-musicians in developing a music curriculum for young children that is comprehensive, exciting, varied, and experience-oriented. The basic philosophical belief underlying the book is that children acquire knowledge through actively exploring their environment. The premise that this is equally true for music is developed throughout the book. Ideas for exploring music throughout the day, as well as in group situations, are presented for each area of music. Although the book is written with the nonmusician in mind, it is equally valuable for the teacher with musical training who is interested in developing a varied and comprehensive music program for young children.

There are a wealth of music- and sound-oriented experiences that are desirable to explore with young children. Unfortunately, many music books written for teachers focus on only one aspect of music, such as singing or movement. Reliance on such texts in planning activities for young children leads to a one-dimensional music curriculum. This book, on the other hand, explores each area of music in depth, relating it to the developmental levels of infants, toddlers, preschool children, and primary children. Whole chapters are devoted to singing, rhythm, instruments, movement, listening, musical concepts, and the Orff system of music instruction. Each chapter discusses ways in which each particular area of music helps children develop. In addition, criteria are suggested for developing and sequencing activities in each area. Specific examples are used to illustrate points discussed in the book.

It is becoming increasingly common for exceptional children to be mainstreamed into classes of normal children from preschool through high school. Therefore, this book includes a chapter on planning music activities for eight types of exceptional children: gifted, orthopedically handicapped, mentally retarded, learning disabled, emotionally disturbed, visually impaired, and speech- and language-impaired. Characteristics of each type of exceptionality are discussed, along with ways in which music can help each type of child developmentally. Specific suggestions are made for planning appropriate music activities for each type of exceptional child, as well as for successfully integrating the child into the music group. Each individual section on exceptionality is self-contained and all-inclusive. Readers may note some repetition among the sections since some problems are common to a variety of exceptionalities. This format was selected so that teachers of a particular type of exceptional child can find all the necessary information in the appropriate section.

Several important theorists come to mind in any discussion of music education—notably Carl Orff, Shinichi Suzuki, and Zoltán Kodály. To understand the work of Suzuki and Kodály, one must have musical training and, in the case of Suzuki, be a string player. Certain aspects of the Orff method, however, can be used by teachers who are nonmusicians. Since the Orff method focuses on creativity and the actual performing of music, and since it encourages growth and development in listening skills, rhythmic awareness, and socialization, I have chosen to focus on it in Chapter 8.

Chapter 4 discusses the use of musical instruments with young children. One notable omission from this chapter is the recorder. The instruments included in the chapter can be used by teachers with no prior musical training. Playing and teaching the recorder, however, does require the ability to read music and some knowledge of recorder technique. Therefore, the recorder was not included in this book.

Knowledge of the various areas of music and skill in planning and implementing specific activities are very helpful to the teacher. In addition, the teacher needs to know how to combine activities from the various areas of music into a complete curriculum or group experience. The final chapter of this book discusses ways to plan complete music experiences. Issues such as the relation of music to the rest of the curriculum, the pacing of group experiences, planning for various developmental age levels, longitudinal planning, and group management skills are discussed fully. Specific sample lessons are included for each age level.

Music is a sound-oriented experience. For this reason many of the examples included in this book are recorded on a cassette tape that accompanies the book. Examples appearing on the tape are indicated by the word **TAPE** in the body of the text.

I am deeply indebted to my husband, Charles J. Moomaw, for his ideas on the musical aspects of this book, his patience, and his hours of work in preparing the manuscript and copying the musical examples. Without his help, I am certain, the book could never have been completed. I also wish to express my heartfelt gratitude to Dr. D. June Sciarra and Anne G. Dorsey, faculty members of the College of Education, University of Cincinnati, for their many insights and suggestions, which have contributed greatly to this book. Appreciation is also due to Allen Otte, faculty member of the College–Conservatory of Music, University of Cincinnati, for his numerous examples of self-made percussion instruments; and to Pamela Runyan for her fine performance for the cassette tape. I also wish to thank my colleagues at the Arlitt Child Development Center, University of Cincinnati, for their ideas, and most particularly the students, whose constant encouragement has been the impetus for this work.

1
Philosophy and Goals

MUSIC IS one of our greatest inheritances as human beings. So global is the human experience of music that it has often been called the universal language of humankind. Music is all around us, a testimony to its great importance for adults. Music is equally important for children from infancy on. Children sing to communicate thoughts and feelings, and their first sounds cover a range of pitch. They sing as they play. They grow silent and intent when they hear unusual sounds. They become quiet and relaxed when they hear soothing sounds. They move their bodies in concert with the sounds they hear. Music is central to the human experience of children, just as it is to adults. For this reason, music should be an important part of the preschool and primary curriculum. There are other reasons as well:

■ Music is a good outlet for children to express and work through their emotions. Clapping, hitting a drum, singing, and jumping are all excellent ways for young children to release both angry feelings and wild, happy ones. There are even specific songs written to deal with specific emotions.[1]

■ Music experiences in the early years further the development of cognition. Through experimenting with how sound is created—whether by producing sounds with their voices or by striking a variety of materials—children form concepts about the nature of sound and music. They also gain a greater awareness of how their actions alter their environment.

■ Music is equally important in developing listening skills. Since children rely so heavily on visual cues, teachers need to encourage them to expand the auditory sense as well. A child must listen very carefully to learn a tune or rhythm, and many children will listen more intently to a song or record than to a story or other language experience. Music activities encourage children to listen much more carefully to the sounds they hear and to form concepts about those sounds.

■ Teachers of young children can also use music effectively to develop gross motor skills and body awareness in young children. Movements that require one side of the body to move independently of the other help children develop laterality; other movements can reinforce awareness of body parts. Finally, moving in many different ways to a variety of music gives children a greater understanding of what they can do with their bodies, helps develop coordination, and encourages imagination.

■ Music also fosters a positive self-image since every child can feel successful in music activities.

PHILOSOPHY

There are four essential questions to consider when exploring music with young children:

1. How should music be approached?
2. When should music be explored?
3. Who should participate?
4. How do developmental stages affect learning about music?

How Should Music Be Approached?

According to Piaget, the child must act on his or her environment in order for cognitive development to proceed.[2] Therefore, children should be given the opportunity to explore all the different aspects of music by concrete means.

In other words, they should be active participants in the music-making process. Children do not learn about sound merely by listening to it. Only by actually producing sounds with a variety of materials, or through physical involvement with the music, do children come to a real understanding of what makes sound and music. Singing, clapping, moving to music, making up music, and playing instruments are some of the many ways in which children can experience music. It is the teacher's responsibility to provide opportunities for the children to make music in these various ways.

Music is all around us all day, and discovery and exploration of sound and music should not be limited to a particular time of the day. The teacher should take the opportunity to explore music with the children whenever it occurs. Children themselves sing spontaneously, tap out little rhythms, and experiment with sounds and movement throughout the day. The teacher should encourage and enjoy these experiences with the children whenever possible.

When Should Music Be Explored?

Todd and Heffernan suggest that one of the important goals of the preschool should be to help children learn to function in a group, and music provides an excellent early group experience.[3] Children can progress from individual experimentation to sharing the experience with another child. Later, children may participate in small groups and eventually in larger groups. The teacher can encourage this growth in social development by providing music experiences as an integral part of the classroom curriculum, in addition to conducting music groups for interested children.

While providing opportunities for experimentation and group participation, the teacher must realize that children will begin making music and participating in groups only when they are ready. Alternative quiet activities can be offered until the child feels comfortable entering the group. Although every child should be given the opportunity to take part in the music-making process, the teacher should not try to force a reluctant child into an activity. Children who do not participate at all during school often recreate the entire experience when they get home.

Who Should Participate?

3

Developmental Stages and Exploring Music

As with other areas of the curriculum, appropriate music activities can be planned only if the teacher understands the developmental stages of the children involved. Although individual differences in the rate of development vary widely, the sequence of development follows a particular pattern. Tables 1.1 through 1.11 show some important behavioral considerations for each stage of development, along with their effect on the child's perception of music. This material is based on the theories of Piaget and Erikson and the writings of Todd and Heffernan.[4]

Table 1.1   Developmental Characteristics, Newborns to One-Month-Olds

Behavioral Characteristics	Music Experiences
Develops trust versus mistrust in environment.[a]	Quiet singing and rocking soothe the baby and formulate trust. Scary sounds avoided.
Responds to stimuli reflexively by moving entire body.	Sound stimuli important. Child reacts to sound by moving entire body.

[a] This behavioral characteristic and its corresponding music experiences are valid through age twenty-four months.

Table 1.2   Developmental Characteristics, One- to Four-Month-Olds

Behavioral Characteristics	Music Experiences
Makes first differentiations. Changes from hearing to listening. Turns head toward stimulus. Follows moving objects with eyes.	Turns head in direction of sound. Follows sound of moving object if it is readily visible.

Table 1.3   Developmental Characteristics, Four- to Eight-Month-Olds

Behavioral Characteristics	Music Experiences
Interested in cause-and-effect relationships. Engages in purposeful activity. Reproduces interesting events. Develops eye-hand coordination.	Hits suspended bells again and again to reproduce the sound.

Table 1.4 Developmental Characteristics, Eight- to Twelve-Month-Olds

Behavioral Characteristics	Music Experiences
Coordinates two schemata.	Hits drum or xylophone with stick.
Anticipates events, exhibits intention.	Claps hands to music.
Knows that objects have stable functions.	Hits instrument to produce a sound.
Imitates actions.	Understands purpose of instrument.

Table 1.5 Developmental Characteristics, Twelve- to Eighteen-Month-Olds

Behavioral Characteristics	Music Experiences
Invents new actions.	Experiments by hitting instrument in different ways with different objects.
Uses trial and error to solve problems.	

Table 1.6 Developmental Characteristics, Eighteen- to Twenty-Four-Month-Olds

Behavioral Characteristics	Music Experiences
Creates new actions through prior thought.	Continues music activity after adult stops.
Imitates actions after person leaves.	

Table 1.7 Developmental Characteristics, Two-Year-Olds

Behavioral Characteristics	Music Experiences
Steps in place.	Enjoys action songs and moving to music.
Pats.	
Runs.	
Increases language.	Can learn short, simple songs.
Has short attention span.	
Attends to spoken words a few at a time.	Activities with short, simple directions.
Develops autonomy, is very curious.	Many opportunities to experiment with instruments and sound.

Table 1.8 Developmental Characteristics, Three-Year-Olds

Behavioral Characteristics	Music Experiences
Jumps, runs, and walks to music.	Special music for special movements.
Has self-control.	Can wait for a turn.
Attentive, has longer attention span.	Longer songs or small group experiences can be planned.
Uses more words.	
Compares two objects.	Experiments with sound comparisons.
Participates in planning.	Suggests words for songs or additional activities.
Initiative emerges.	Choices important along with an opportunity to try out their own ideas.

Table 1.9 Developmental Characteristics, Four-Year-Olds

Behavioral Characteristics	Music Experiences
Has better motor control.	May begin skipping.
Interested in rules.	Rule songs and games appropriate.
Plans ahead with adults.	Children can make suggestions for music activities.
Likes to imagine.	Adds words to songs.
	Creates songs on instruments.
	Dramatic movements.

Table 1.10 Developmental Characteristics, Five- and Six-Year-Olds

Behavioral Characteristics	Music Experiences
Has motor control.	Able to sit longer.
Likes to have rules.	Enjoys songs and dances with rules.
	Specific rhythm patterns.

Table 1.11 Developmental Characteristics, Seven- and Eight-Year-Olds

Behavioral Characteristics	Music Experiences
Begins to read written symbols.	May be able to read words to songs.
Concerned with rules.	Rule dances and songs especially
Cooperation and competition.	valued.
Logical thought processes emerge.	Better able to differentiate reality from fantasy.
Seriation—compares more than two objects after first object removed.	Can compare three or more sounds or pitches.

What, then, should be the goals of music experiences with young children? **GOALS**

- Children should have many opportunities to explore music through their voices, through their body movements, and through making sounds with instruments.
- They should have opportunities to express emotions through music.
- They should gain increased understanding of what makes different kinds of sounds.
- They should have opportunities to expand listening skills.
- They should develop increased awareness of body image and self-identity.
- They should develop increased enjoyment of music.
- They should explore their own creativity in music.
- Children should have experiences that reflect their developmental needs.
- They should have opportunities for group participation.

The teacher can achieve these broad goals by providing a wide variety of musical experiences and allowing for as much input from the children as possible. The teacher will need to provide for both individual experimentation and group participation, and the music curriculum should encompass songs, rhythm, instruments, movement, listening activities, and musical concepts.

Activities   What, specifically, do each of the six aforementioned activities offer the child?

Songs   Children love to sing. From infancy on they experiment with their voices and the sounds they make. This is one reason for providing many opportunities for singing in the classroom. Actually performing the music increases children's enjoyment and understanding of it. Another reason to include songs in the curriculum is that children need to experiment with the different sounds they can make with their voices, and singing gives them an opportunity to do so. Listening to songs and learning them improves children's listening skills, and singing provides a great emotional release for children just as it does for adults. Perhaps most important, using their own voices gives children the concrete experience necessary for understanding what makes vocal sound.

Rhythm   Rhythmic activities give children concrete means to explore and perceive the pulse, relative duration, and flow of sound and speech. Later they will build on these skills as they learn to divide and sound out words. Also, children from infants on love to experiment with rhythms. One of the first games babies delight in is pat-a-cake, which is undoubtedly an elementary exploration of rhythm.

Instruments   Children learn many things through experimenting with instruments. They learn that different kinds of materials make different sounds. They discover that the way they play the instrument—how hard or soft, how fast or slow—also affects the sound. They also learn how the size of an instrument affects the sound. For instance, big drums sound lower than little drums, and the long bars on the xylophone sound lower than the short bars. Concrete experience with instruments helps children develop the concepts necessary for later understanding and enjoyment in listening to music. Finally, playing instruments gives children an opportunity to create new sounds and express themselves through the sounds they make.

Through movement, children learn about their bodies and how they function. Children explore movement naturally, as one can readily observe by watching them as they play. Dramatizing animals or objects allows children to take on another role, to pretend, and thereby to extend their imaginations. Children's creativity is also developed by allowing them to move as the music makes them feel. Finally, the teacher can work on laterality and coordination through carefully planned movement experiences.

Movement

Listening involves purposeful hearing, and listening activities help children develop finer auditory discrimination. Teachers can help children increase their listening skills by suggesting specific things to listen for and encouraging them to listen carefully to sounds they hear throughout the day. Teachers can also help children understand how listening to different kinds of music makes them feel.

Listening

Experience with musical concepts such as fast-slow, high-low, and up-down helps children develop auditory discrimination and listening skills. Such experience also helps in the formulation of concepts and thereby increases children's understanding of sound and music.

Musical Concepts

Chapters 2 through 7 discuss in detail each of the six aforementioned areas.

Preparing musical experiences for young children, no matter how spontaneous these activities may seem, takes prior thought and preparation if successful experiences are to be provided and curriculum goals met. Chapter 8 discusses one specific system of music instruction, the Carl Orff method, and suggests ways in which the nonmusician can use the Orff method in planning and implementing music activities in the classroom. Chapter 9 discusses ways of planning and implementing music activities with exceptional children. Finally, Chapter 10 describes in detail how the teacher should approach planning for the total music curriculum.

Planning Music Activities for Children

1. A good source for songs dealing with feelings is Fred Rogers, *Mister Rogers' Song Book* (New York: Random House, 1970).

NOTES

2. Barry J. Wadsworth, *Piaget's Theory of Cognitive Development* (New York: David McKay, 1971), p. 22.

3. Vivian Edmiston Todd and Helen Heffernan, *The Years before School* (New York: Macmillan, 1970), p. 491.

4. Wadsworth, *Piaget's Theory*; Erik K. Erikson, *Childhood and Society* (New York: W. W. Norton, 1963); Todd and Heffernan, *Years before School*, p. 36.

SELECTED BIBLIOGRAPHY

Erikson, Erik K. *Childhood and Society.* New York: W. W. Norton, 1963.

Forman, George E., and Kuschner, David S. *The Child's Construction of Knowledge: Piaget for Teaching Children.* Monterrey, Calif.: Brooks/Cole, 1977.

Hymes, James L., Jr. *The Child under Six.* Englewood Cliffs, N.J.: Prentice-Hall, 1969.

Leeper, Sarah Hammond; Skipper, Dora Sikes; and Witherspoon, Ralph L. *Good Schools for Young Children,* 4th ed. New York: Macmillan, 1979.

Pulaski, Mary Ann Spencer. *Understanding Piaget.* New York: Harper and Row, 1971.

——. *Your Baby's Mind and How It Grows: Piaget's Theory for Parents.* New York: Harper and Row, 1978.

Stone, L. Joseph, and Church, Joseph. *Childhood and Adolescence,* 4th ed. New York: Random House, 1979.

Todd, Vivian Edmiston, and Heffernan, Helen. *The Years before School.* New York: Macmillan, 1971.

Wadsworth, Barry J. *Piaget's Theory of Cognitive Development.* New York: David McKay, 1971.

2
Songs

SONGS ARE an integral part of the musical experience of young children. Most children sing spontaneously from an early age whether or not they are ever formally taught a song. Since singing is an important means of expression for young children, it should be an important part of the preschool and primary curriculum. Teachers of young children, then, need to consider what criteria they will use in selecting songs, what types of songs are appropriate, where they can find songs, and what techniques they will use to teach songs.

CRITERIA FOR SELECTING SONGS

The teacher needs to consider several important factors when selecting songs for young children: the length of the song, the repetitiveness of the melody and words, the content or subject matter of the song, the range of the melody, and how well the song coordinates with the rest of the curriculum.

Length

The first thing a teacher should consider when selecting a song for young children is length. A song that is too long and complex will not hold the attention of the children, and

11

they will be unable to sing it. If a song is too short and simple, however, the children may lose interest quickly.

Toddlers need very short, simple songs. "Rock-a-Bye" (Example 2.1) is a good song for toddlers because it is very brief and almost invites them to move their bodies to the sound of the words.

Three-year-olds are ready for slightly longer songs. Although they may still enjoy some short ones like "Rock-a-Bye," in general they need the challenge of songs that are a little longer and more complex, such as "Swish, Swish, Swish" (Example 2.2). Another song of appropriate length for three-year-olds is "Raining" (Example 2.3).

Four- and five-year-olds are usually ready for still longer and more complicated songs. Some three-year-olds will be ready for these longer songs too, and some four-year-olds may not. The dynamics of each group of children is different, so the teacher must assess what level of song the class is ready for. In general, however, four- or five-year-olds enjoy the challenge of longer songs such as "Thunder" (Example 2.4) and "Our Guinea Pig" (Example 2.5).

Primary-age children can learn progressively longer songs since their language and retentive memory are better developed. A song such as "We're Going to Plant a Garden" (Example 2.6) can be taught to first- and second-graders with the verses added gradually. Some second-graders and many third-graders may be able to read the words.

Repetition

Another important factor to consider when selecting songs for young children is the repetition of melody and words. Young children love repetition, and songs with repetitive melody and words are much easier for them to learn. "Autumn Leaves" (Example 2.7), written by a college student, is a good song for young children because it repeats both melody and words.

Content

A very important consideration in selecting songs is their content. Some songs commonly taught to preschool children are inappropriate for their stage of development and deal with subject matter that is completely foreign to the young child. Many nursery rhymes fit into this category. For example, "Hey Diddle, Diddle," a song we adults grew up with, may evoke fond memories of childhood, but the words are misleading

Example 2.1
ROCK-A-BYE

Original key: A-flat

Laura Bryant

Rock-a-bye, lul-la-bye. Dol-ly go to sleep.

Source: Laura Bryant, *Sentence Songs for Little Singers*
(Cincinnati: Willis Music Company, 1935). Used by permission, Willis
Music Co., Inc.

Example 2.2
SWISH, SWISH, SWISH

Sally Moomaw

Swish, swish, swish, I'm a lit-tle fish,

Swim-ming through the wa-ter, Swish, swish, swish.

Copyright ©1972, 1980 by Sally Coup Moomaw.

Example 2.3
RAINING

Original key: E-flat

Ethel Crowninshield

It's rain-ing on the side-walk, It's rain-ing on the tree,

I'll go out with my rain-coat on and let it rain on me.

Source: Ethel Crowninshield, *New Songs and Games* (Boston: Boston
Music Company, 1941). Used by permission of the copyright owner: THE
BOSTON MUSIC COMPANY, Boston, MA 02216

and confusing to preschool children. Since they are still trying to separate reality from fantasy, they typically do not appreciate the humor of the cow jumping over the moon and the dog laughing.[1] After hearing this song, one three-year-old boy asked for the moon to be brought down so that he could jump over it, too.

Many songs deal with subject matter that is actually frightening to young children. One such song, by a well-known children's songwriter, tells of robbers knocking on the door and of being hit over the head with a rolling pin. This song may be an important part of folk culture and humorous to adults, but preschool and some primary-age children are too young to appreciate the humor and may be disturbed by the notion of robbers coming to their doors.

Many frightening songs surface around Halloween. Songs about witches and goblins are frightening to young children who are not yet certain that such things do not exist. There are some appropriate Halloween songs for young children,

TAPE

Example 2.4
THUNDER

Sally Moomaw

I looked up in the sky and saw a big, black cloud,

And then I heard a rum-ble that was loud, loud, loud.

My dad-dy said,"Don't wor-ry 'bout the roar, roar, roar,

It on-ly means that soon the rain will pour, pour, pour."

Example 2.5
OUR GUINEA PIG

Sally Moomaw

We have a lit- tle gui- nea pig. She's

soft and fat but not ve- ry big. Her

fur is black and white and kind of fan- cy, and

we have de- ci-ded to call her Nan- cy. We

love to pet our gui- nea pig. We

love to watch her eat and watch her dig.

When we hold her may- be we can

hear our lit- tle gui- nea pig go ee- ee- ee.

Copyright ©1978, 1980 by Sally Coup Moomaw.

however. An example of a nonfrightening Halloween song for young children is "Pumpkin" (Example 2.8).

Older children may enjoy a longer, more detailed song like "Making a Jack-o-Lantern" (Example 2.9). This song,

TAPE
(1st & 5th verses)

Example 2.6
WE'RE GOING TO PLANT A GARDEN

Sally Moomaw

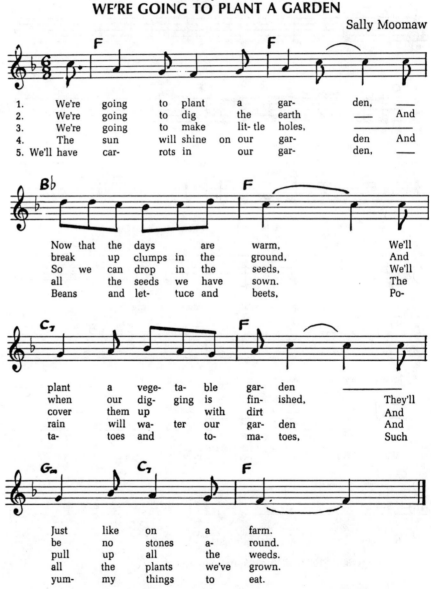

1. We're going to plant a gar- den, ___
2. We're going to dig the earth ___ And
3. We're going to make lit-tle holes, _____
4. The sun will shine on our gar- den And
5. We'll have car- rots in our gar- den, ___

Now that the days are warm, We'll
break up clumps in the ground, And
So we can drop in the seeds, We'll
all the seeds we have sown. The
Beans and let- tuce and beets, Po-

plant a vege- ta- ble gar- den _____ They'll
when our dig- ging is fin- ished, And
cover them up with dirt And
rain will wa- ter our gar- den And
ta- toes and to- ma- toes, Such

Just like on a farm.
be no stones a- round.
pull up all the weeds.
all the plants we've grown.
yum- my things to eat.

16   Copyright ©1980 by Sally Coup Moomaw.

which emphasizes the process involved in making a jack-o-lantern, helps dispel the idea that a pumpkin can magically transform itself into a jack-o-lantern. This is particularly true if the children have examined a pumpkin and carved one in the classroom.

If a class is intrigued with witches so that the teacher feels a need to talk about witches on Halloween, a song such as "Witches" (Example 2.10) might be selected. This song emphasizes that witches are not real but may be fun to pretend about.

Example 2.7
AUTUMN LEAVES

TAPE
(1st & 2nd verses)

Gail Westendorf Klayman

2. Autumn leaves are turning colors . . .
3. Autumn leaves are dancing . . .
4. Autumn leaves are being raked . . .

Used by kind permission of Gail Westendorf Klayman.

Example 2.8
PUMPKIN

TAPE

Original key: B-flat

Katherine O. Williams

Source: Laura Bryant, *More Sentence Songs for Little Singers* (Cincinnati: Willis Music Company, 1939). Used by permission, Willis Music Co., Inc.

Example 2.9
MAKING A JACK-O-LANTERN

Sally Moomaw

We bought a pump-kin so big and round And

cut the top right off his crown, But

when we looked in-side, The first thing that we spied Were

hun-dreds of slip- p'ry seeds.

2. We put our hands in and felt the goo.
   It was so slimy everyone said OO,
   And then we cut a face
   And put his crown in place
   And took turns saying "boo."

3. Our jack-o-lantern was quite a sight,
   Especially when we added a light.
   His eyes were glowing bright,
   He looked like such a fright,
   Just right for Halloween night.

What does constitute good content in a song for young children? First, the song should be about things they are familiar with. Songs about children, families, the weather, transportation, and community workers deal with relevant subject matter for young children. For example, the song "Thunder" (Example 2.4) readily appeals to young children because it deals with something they are familiar with and struggling to understand.

Example 2.10
WITCHES

Original key: F minor   Richard Berg

I know there are no wit-ches that go rid-ing through the air,

but I pre-tend on Hal-lo-ween that they are real-ly there.

Source: From *Sharing Music*, Level K of the MUSIC FOR YOUNG AMERICANS series by Richard Berg et al., Copyright ©1966. Reprinted by permission of American Book Company.

Songs about feelings are also appropriate for young children. *Mister Rogers' Songbook* contains many songs dealing with the feelings of young children, but since the songs are somewhat difficult to sing, they are best suited for primary-age children.[2] The familiar song "If You're Happy and You Know It" (Example 2.11) is appropriate for young children of all ages.

Songs that encourage children to use their imaginations are also appropriate. A song like "Clouds" (Example 2.12) stimulates young imaginations. The words were composed by a three-year-old as he watched the sky. Each child can add something different to the song.

Many songs have lyrics that can be altered by the children. For example, in "Building Blocks" (Example 2.13), the teacher can ask the children what things they like to build with the blocks, and then add their responses to the song.

When selecting songs for young children, the teacher also **Range** needs to consider the *range* of the melody—how high and low the song goes. Since young children typically have rather high voices, in general the songs should not go below middle C:

Example 2.11
IF YOU'RE HAPPY AND YOU KNOW IT

Traditional

If you're hap- py and you know it clap your hands.

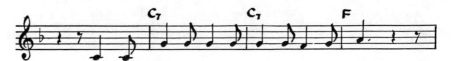

If you're hap- py and you know it clap your hands.

If you're hap- py and you know it then your face will sure- ly

show it, If you're hap- py and you know it clap your hands.

2. If you're mad and you know it stamp your feet.
   If you're mad and you know it stamp your feet.
   If you're mad and you know it, then your face will
      surely show it,
   If you're mad and you know it, stamp your feet.

3. If you're sad and you know it wipe your eyes.
   If you're sad and you know it wipe your eyes.
   If you're sad and you know it, then your face will
      surely show it,
   If you're sad and you know it wipe your eyes.

4. If you're sleepy and you know it close your eyes.
   If you're sleepy and you know it close your eyes.
   If you're sleepy and you know it, then your face
      will surely show it,
   If you're sleepy and you know it close your eyes.

5. Repeat verse 1,

Example 2.12
CLOUDS

TAPE
(1st & 2nd verses)

Peter Moomaw

Sally Moomaw

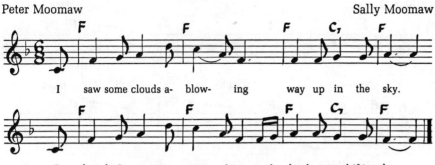

I saw some clouds a- blow- ing way up in the sky.

I thought I saw so ma- ny things as the clouds went drifting by.

2. I thought I saw a horsy way up in the sky,
   I thought I saw a horsy as the clouds went drifting
      by.

3. I thought I saw a great big crane way up in the
      sky,
   I thought I saw a great big crane as the clouds went
      drifting by.

4. The sky man drove the crane away way up in the
      sky,
   I pretended he drove the crane away as the clouds
      went drifting by.

Copyright ©1979, 1980 by Sally Coup Moomaw.

They also have trouble singing up very high, however, so
high C or D is as high as the song should go:

c   d

Many songs for young children do lie in this range.

   Young children can most easily sing songs that move by
step:

Example 2.13
BUILDING BLOCKS

Mary Francis   Daniel Hooley

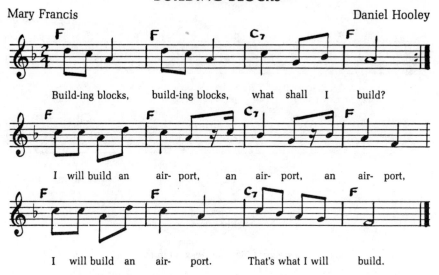

Build-ing blocks,   build-ing blocks,   what   shall   I   build?

I will build an   air- port,   an   air- port,   an   air- port,

I will build an   air-   port.   That's what I will   build.

Source: From *Sharing Music*, Level K of the MUSIC FOR YOUNG
AMERICANS series by Richard Berg et al., Copyright ©1966. Reprinted
by permission of American Book Company.

or have small skips between the notes:

Songs with large skips are difficult for them to sing:

Primary-age children can sing large skips a little more easily
than younger children can. "It Was Snow" (Example 2.14) is
easy to sing because the notes move by step or with small
skips. The range also lies between the two Cs:

Example 2.14
IT WAS SNOW

Sally Moomaw

It looked like balls of cot-ton, It looked like coo-kie dough,

It looked like my white blan-ket, It was snow, snow, snow.

Copyright ©1978, 1980 by Sally Coup Moomaw.

"Jack and Jill" (Example 2.15), on the other hand, has many large skips and is thus difficult to sing.

Relevance

Songs take on added meaning when they are coordinated with the rest of the curriculum. For example, if the class has taken a trip to the zoo or is planning one, songs about zoo animals would be of added interest to the children. If the class has been talking about transportation, then songs about transportation would help reinforce concepts of vehicles and where they travel. Not every song needs to coordinate with the rest of the curriculum, but it is good planning to include some that do.

Example 2.15
JACK AND JILL

Traditional

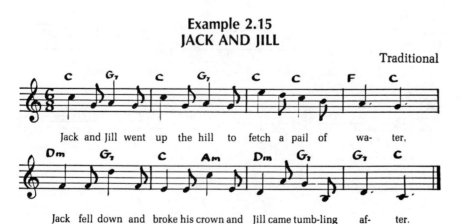

Jack and Jill went up the hill to fetch a pail of wa-ter,

Jack fell down and broke his crown and Jill came tumb-ling af-ter.

In this chapter we have discussed what makes a song appropriate or inappropriate for use with young children. Several special categories of songs bear further discussion, however: movement songs with directions, free movement songs, finger plays, and echo songs.

Movement Songs with Directions

Many songs for young children fit into this category. In these songs the words tell the singer what to do. Two examples are "The Hokey Pokey" (Example 2.16) and "Put Your Finger on Your Nose" (Example 2.17).

Young children enjoy songs like these, and songs with directions help teach important listening skills. Many teachers rely on the record player when teaching these movement songs. Although following directions from a record is

Example 2.16
THE HOKEY POKEY

Traditional

You put your right hand in, you put your right hand out, you put your right hand in and you shake it all a-bout. You do the ho-key po-key and you turn your-self a-round. That's what it's all a- bout.

2. left hand
3. right foot
4. left foot
5. whole self

a good skill for young children to acquire, it is much easier for them to learn the song if the teacher first sings the song and waits until later to use the record. This permits the teacher to vary the speed and to maintain eye contact with the children.

Free Movement Songs

Free movement songs deal with subject matter that is easy for the children to reenact or have music that encourages them to dramatize the sounds. These songs are especially valuable for use with young children because they encourage the children to think imaginatively and use their bodies creatively. For example, songs about animals encourage the children to take on the role of the animal and move their bodies as the animal does. Children often respond to songs about wind and rain by swaying or falling.

The teacher can make songs into action songs by simply asking the children to act out what they hear in the song. For example, "Autumn Leaves" (Example 2.7) makes a

Example 2.17
PUT YOUR FINGER ON YOUR NOSE

Traditional

Put your fin-ger on your nose, then your toes.
Put your fin-ger on your nose, then your toes.
Put your fin-ger on your nose, Put your fin-ger on your nose, Put your fin-ger on your nose, then your toes.

wonderful creative movement song as the children act out all the things the leaves do.

If possible, the teacher should be an encouraging observer and not set a model for the children. If the children seem to be having trouble acting out a song, they may not have had enough experience with the subject matter. Dropping a real leaf while they watch or giving them leaves to drop might overcome this problem for a song such as "Autumn Leaves."

Some children are very eager to act out songs; others prefer to watch. The teacher should not try to force children to do creative movement. The way to build positive self-concepts in children and a real enjoyment of music is to allow them to observe the other children for as long as they wish and gradually, on their own initiative, begin to join in themselves. Some children will gradually become more at ease and begin to act out songs. Others never will, and that is fine, too. Creative movement to songs is dealt with in greater detail in Chapter 5.

Example 2.18
THE EENCY WEENCY SPIDER

Traditional

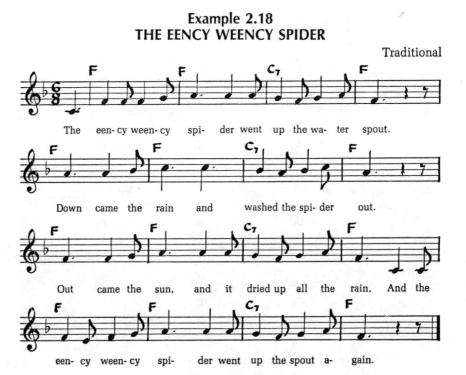

Finger plays are quite popular in the preschool classroom. **Finger Plays** This category includes songs such as "The Eency Weency Spider" (Example 2.18) that the children act out with their fingers. Perhaps one reason children enjoy finger plays so much is that they can actually see the action they are performing, unlike whole body movements, which they are unable to view.

Rather than rely solely on the common finger plays, teachers can encourage children to make up their own finger movements to songs they know. "Snowflakes" (Example 2.19) for example, was not written as a finger play, but children could act it out with their hands as well as their bodies. Additional verses could be added to the song with more motions to imitate—for example:

> The snowflakes are blowing . . .
> The snowflakes are dancing . . .
> The snowflakes are swirling . . .
> The snowflakes are melting . . .

Another type of song is one in which the teacher sings a short **Echo Songs** phrase and the children sing it back, or the teacher sings a question and the children sing the answer. As children develop, the first interval (distance between two notes) they

Example 2.19
SNOWFLAKES

Nina M. Kenagy
Francis M. Arnold

Source: Nina M. Kenagy and Francis M. Arnold, *Musical Experiences of Little Children* (Cincinnati: Willis Music Company, 1932). Used by permission, Willis Music Co., Inc.

sing is the falling minor third.[3] This is the interval we hear when they call another child's name or sing a little taunt:

TAPE

Su- san   Na na na na na

This interval is the easiest one for children to sing, so it is a good one to start with for echoing. The teacher can begin by singing a word and having the children sing it back:

tur- tle   tur- tle

Alternatively, the teacher can sing a phrase asking a child to sing back his or her own name:

TAPE

Sing me your name   Sha- ron

Some children may decide to elaborate. One child sang:

I'm Sha-ron and I'm   neat!

Children often have trouble understanding the concept of echoing. They may want to sing along with the teacher and not understand that they have to listen first and then answer. An assistant or parent can help demonstrate the concept by echoing the teacher. Once the children are accustomed to echoing, the teacher can make the echo songs longer and thereby extend the children's listening skills. Echoing should begin simply, however, with just a single word to echo.

Echoing is too difficult for most two-year-olds. Children three to five years old can begin to echo, but the teacher should expect wide individual differences in their ability to do so. Most primary-age children are ready to begin simple echos.

WHERE TO FIND SONGS

There are many songbooks for young children. Teachers can find them in libraries and bookstores or order them through catalogs (see the Selected Bibliography at the end of this chapter). In looking through these books, the teacher will need to evaluate each song carefully on the basis of the criteria suggested in this chapter.

One good source of songs is making them up. Most people do not believe they can compose a song, but it is not difficult. Start by deciding what the song will be about, next write the words, and finally sing some melodies to go with the words until you find one that seems to fit. "Autumn Leaves" (Example 2.7) was written by a student teacher. "The Hippopotamus" (Example 2.20) was written by a preschool teacher.

Example 2.20
THE HIPPOPOTAMUS

Patricia Bevan

The hip- po- po- ta- mus walks with a thud, He

likes to roll a- round in the mud, He

o- pens up his mouth so wide that

you can see his teeth in- side.

Used by kind permission of Patricia Bevan.

An easy way to compose songs is to take a preexisting melody and add new words to it. For instance, the tune of "Here We Go Round the Mulberry Bush" (Example 2.21) lends itself to a variety of words. Here are four different ways to use the same tune. In the first version, "Shapes," children guessed the names of the shapes that the teacher held up:

TAPE

Can you guess the shape I have, the shape I have, the shape I have?
Can you guess the shape I have at school with me today?

In another version, "Transportation," the children thought of various transportation vehicles and added them to the song along with whether they went on land, in the air, or in the water:

I can ride in an automobile, an automobile, an automobile,
I can ride in an automobile. It goes on the land.

A third version was created spontaneously for a group of children who were eagerly awaiting their turn in a large-motor development room. The children thought of all the things they wanted to do when they got to the muscle room and added these to the song, "Muscle Room Time." This activity transformed what could have been a time of pandemonium into a quiet, delightful transition.

Soon we will go to the muscle room, the muscle room, the muscle room,
Soon we will go to the muscle room, and have a lot of fun.

Children often compose their own songs and are delighted if the teacher sings along with them or remembers their song and sings it at a later time. "This Is the Way You Make a Train," a final version of the tune "Here We Go Round the

Example 2.21
HERE WE GO ROUND THE MULBERRY BUSH
Traditional

Here we go round the mul-ber-ry bush, the mul-ber-ry bush, the mul-ber-ry bush, Here we go round the mul-ber-ry bush, so ear-ly in the morn-ing.

Mulberry Bush," was composed by a two-and-a-half-year-old as he played with his blocks.

1. This is the way you make a train, make a train, make a train.
    This is the way you make a train, just like this.

2. First you put the engine on . . .
3. Then you put the hopper on . . .
4. Then you put the boxcar on . . .
5. Then you put the caboose on . . .

TEACHING SONGS

There are three ways to teach songs to children: the whole song method, the part song method, and the use of recordings. In general, the whole song method or a combination of whole song and part song methods are most effective with young children.

31

Whole Song Method   The *whole song method* simply means that the teacher sings the entire song several times until the children know it. This method is recommended for young children because they tend to lose continuity and forget parts of a song when the teacher breaks it up. Obviously, the whole song method works best with shorter songs. Sometimes the children can begin singing certain parts of the song while the teacher sings the entire song. This works well with a song that has a refrain, like "I'm a Person" (Example 2.22). The children can begin singing the "No I'm not" part while the teacher sings the rest of the words.

Part Song Method   In the *part song method* the teacher breaks the song into lines and teaches one line or phrase at a time. This method is generally not recommended for young children because they cannot keep the content of the whole song in mind when it is broken up. Toddlers and preschool children especially have this problem. Some songs for primary children are so long, however, that the teacher may need to sing just one line at a time. "I Saw a Little Squirrel" (Example 2.23) is such a song.

Clearly, this song is too long and complex for the children to learn as a whole unless the teacher sings it countless times. This is the type of song for which the part song method is useful.

The teacher begins by singing the entire song so that the children know what the song is about. Next the teacher sings the first line of the song, "I saw a little squirrel / It ran away from me," several times until the children are able to join in. The teacher then sings the second line, "I chased it down the sidewalk / But it scampered up a tree," until the children can sing that line too. Now the teacher sings the first two lines of the song together, repeating these two lines until the children can join in. This is a good place to stop if the children seem to be getting tired. The song can be continued the next day. If the teacher does stop at this point, the whole sequence of instruction will have to be repeated when the song is resumed the next day. (Of course, it will probably take much less time to cover these lines on the second day.) When the children can sing the first two lines together, the next step is for the teacher to sing the third line, "I peered up through the leaves with my head bent back," until the children can sing it. Then the teacher sings the fourth line, "I saw it eat a nut, with a crack, crack, crack!" until the children can also

Example 2.22
I'M A PERSON

TAPE
(1st verse only)

Lois Raebeck

Are you a box? NO I'M NOT! Are you a ball? NO I'M NOT!

Are you the floor or are you the wall?

NO I'M NOT! NO I'M NOT! I'M A PER-SON AND THAT'S A LOT!

2. Are you a coat? NO I'M NOT!
   Are you a hat? NO I'M NOT!
   Are you a dog or are you a cat?
   NO I'M NOT! NO I'M NOT! I'M A PERSON AND
   THAT'S A LOT!

3. Are you the wind? NO I'M NOT!
   Are you the air? NO I'M NOT!
   Are you a horse or are you a bear?
   NO I'M NOT! NO I'M NOT! I'M A PERSON AND
   THAT'S A LOT!

4. Are you a train? NO I'M NOT!
   Or an airplane? NO I'M NOT!
   Are you the snow or are you the rain?
   NO I'M NOT! NO I'M NOT! I'M A PERSON AND
   THAT'S A LOT!

5. Are you a tree? NO I'M NOT!
   Or a bumblebee? NO I'M NOT!
   Are you the lock or are you the key?
   NO I'M NOT! NO I'M NOT! I'M A PERSON AND
   THAT'S A LOT!

6. Are you a clock? NO I'M NOT!
   Or a warm sock? NO I'M NOT!
   Are you a stone or are you a rock?
   NO I'M NOT! NO I'M NOT! I'M A PERSON AND
   THAT'S A LOT!

Example 2.23
I SAW A LITTLE SQUIRREL

Sally Moomaw

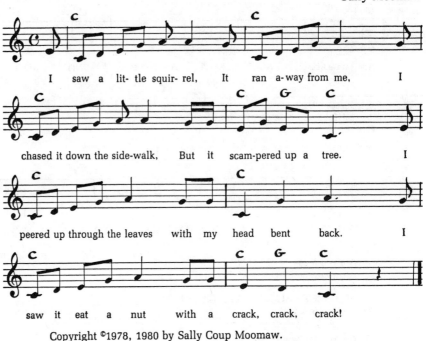

I saw a lit-tle squir-rel, It ran a-way from me, I

chased it down the side-walk, But it scam-pered up a tree. I

peered up through the leaves with my head bent back. I

saw it eat a nut with a crack, crack, crack!

sing this. Next the teacher sings the third and fourth lines together, repeating these two lines until the children can join in. Finally, the teacher sings the entire song and then repeats it so that the children can sing along. On subsequent days the children will probably know the song well enough to start out by singing the entire song. Table 2.1 is a diagram of the part song method.

Sometimes the teacher can combine the whole song and part song methods by singing the whole song but then repeating a few difficult lines until the children remember them. If either the part song method or the combination method is used, the teacher should always start and end by singing the entire song.

Recording Method   Children can also learn songs by listening to records. It is much easier, however, for the teacher to hold their attention by singing the song. The teacher's singing also encourages

Table 2.1 Diagram of the Part Song Method

T = teacher	C = Children
T	entire song
T	line 1
T and C	line 1
T	line 2
T and C	line 2
T	lines 1 and 2
T and C	lines 1 and 2
T	line 3
T and C	line 3
T	line 4
T and C	line 4
T	lines 3 and 4
T and C	lines 3 and 4
T	entire song
T and C	entire song

the children to sing more than does the inanimate record player.

Regardless of the method used, the teacher needs to know the song thoroughly before attempting to teach it. A teacher who has to keep looking at the song cannot focus adequate attention on the children. By knowing the song well beforehand, the teacher can sing and still look at all the children.

ENHANCING SONGS

Teachers can do several things to make songs more interesting for the children. They can accompany the song or have the children accompany it. They can also find ways to extend or alter the song.

Accompanying Songs

Songs are greatly enriched if the teacher can supply a little accompaniment while singing. A teacher who can play the piano will certainly want to play for the class from time to time. The piano, however, is not an ideal instrument for regularly accompanying songs with young children because its bulk imposes a substantial physical barrier between the children and the teacher. Instruments such as the autoharp or the guitar are preferable since they can be held on the lap; this allows the teacher to maintain close contact with the children. The autoharp, which can be played by anyone, with or without any music background, is an excellent investment for any school. (See Chapter 4 for more information on accompanying instruments.)

It is more difficult for the children to hear the melody of a song when it is accompanied. Therefore, the teacher may wish to play the song without accompaniment until the children are familiar with it.

Extending Songs

Once the children know a song well, the teacher may wish to vary it. This can be done by adding rhythm instruments, accompanying instruments, or creative movement. These activities are discussed in Chapters 4 and 5.

SONGS THROUGHOUT THE DAY

Songs should not be relegated strictly to music time. Many children sing spontaneously throughout the day, and the teacher should take advantage of this and sing with them. The song "This Is the Way You Make a Train," cited earlier in this chapter, was composed by a child as he played.

Teachers can also sing spontaneously at various times during the day. The children usually delight in this. For example, if the children are busy with a cooking activity, the teacher might wish to sing a song like "The Baker Man" (Example 2.24) and alter the words to fit each given activity. Verses such as the following could be added to follow the sequence of the cooking activity:

> See the busy baker girl
> Sifting flour as fast as she can.
>
> See the busy baker boy,
> Pouring in raisins as fast as he can.
>
> See the hungry baker children,
> Eating cookies as fast as they can.

Similarly, a song such as "Hammering" (Example 2.25) might be sung while children work at the woodworking bench.

Example 2.24
THE BAKER MAN

Original Key: A-flat   Louise Hitchcock

See the lit- tle   ba- ker man

Mak- ing cakes as   fast as he can.

Source: Laura Bryant, *More Sentence Songs for Little Singers* (Cincinnati: Willis Music Company, 1939). Used by permission, Willis Music Co., Inc.

Example 2.25
HAMMERING

Sally Moomaw

Tap,   tap,   rat- a- tat- a- tat.

Ham- mer- ing takes   so much strength, but

Tap,   tap,   rat- a- tat- a- tat.

I think I am   strong!

Copyright ©1980 by Sally Coup Moomaw.

Songs can be a real aid to the teacher at different times during the day, such as the transition between activities or cleanup. Singing captures the children's attention and helps make a confusing time or an unpleasant task more enjoyable. Earlier in this chapter the example was given of converting "Here We Go Round the Mulberry Bush" into a transition song for children waiting to go to a large-muscle room. The same tune could be used for a variety of transitions, since almost any short sentence can be made to fit the melody. For example, if the teacher needed to get the class ready to go outside, this version of the song might be used:

Now it's time to go outside, go outside, go outside,
Now it's time to go outside, so let's put on our coats.

Copyright © 1979, 1980 by Sally Coup Moomaw.

Singing is so soothing to most children that the teacher may be able to encourage cautious children to try new activities by singing about them. For example, a five-year-old boy in one class was afraid to try any large-muscle activity. The teacher felt he needed to develop himself in this area, but she was reluctant to force him. One day some children were rocking in a boat, and the teacher began singing "Row, Row, Row Your Boat." To her surprise, the child she was concerned about came over and climbed into the boat with the other children. The teacher hypothesized that her singing may have put him at ease and made him feel comfortable joining in. She therefore began singing as children did other large-muscle activities. Sure enough, the cautious child joined in and was soon climbing and jumping.

SUMMARY

Songs are an important addition to the preschool curriculum, not only during music time, but throughout the day. Carefully selected songs can greatly enrich the child's school experience.

It is very important for the teacher to evaluate a song carefully before using it. The age and interests of the class have an important bearing on which songs are selected. The teacher might also consider the following questions:

- Is the song long enough to hold the class's attention but not so long that they will lose interest?
- Is there enough repetition of melody and words to make the song easy to remember?
- Does the content of the song deal with things familiar to the children, and does it carefully separate reality from imagination?
- Is the tune easy for children to sing—neither too high nor too low?
- Does the song coordinate well with the rest of the curriculum?

The teacher can vary the music program by using special songs. Children enjoy songs that give directions for movement; they also like to create movements to fit songs. Finger plays and echo songs are other types of special songs that create variety in the music program.

Teachers can locate songs by consulting music books in the library or at bookstores. They can also create their own songs and encourage the children to make up songs.

When teaching a song, the teacher must decide whether to use the whole song method, the part song method, or the recording method. For most songs, the whole song method works best. For very long songs, however, the part song method or the combination approach may be necessary. Occasionally the children may enjoy learning a song from a record. Once the children know a song well, the teacher may wish to accompany it or extend it by adding rhythm instruments or movement.

NOTES

1. The idea that imagination is rooted in reality is expressed in James L. Hymes, Jr., *The Child under Six* (Englewood Cliffs, N.J.: Prentice Hall, 1969), p. 184.

2. Fred Rogers, *Mister Rogers' Songbook* (New York: Random House, 1970).

3. Erzsébet Szönyi, *Kodály's Principles in Practice*, trans. John Weissman (London: Boosey and Hawkes Music Publishers, 1973), p. 28.

SELECTED BIBLIOGRAPHY

Boesel, Ann Sterling. *Singing with Peter and Patsy.* New York: Oxford University Press, 1944.

Bryant, Laura. *Sentence Songs for Little Singers*. Cincinnati: Willis Music Company, 1935.

——. *More Sentence Songs for Little Singers*. Cincinnati: Willis Music Company, 1939.

Bryant, Laura, and Ruff, Edna. *Still More Sentence Songs*. Cincinnati: Willis Music Company, 1945.

Choate, Robert A.; Kjelson, Lee; Berg, Richard C.; and Troth, Eugene W. *Enjoying Music*. New Dimensions in Music. New York: American Book Company, 1970.

Coleman, Satis N., and Thorn, Alice G. *Singing Time*. New York: John Day Company, 1929.

Crowninshield, Ethel. *New Songs and Games*. Boston: Boston Music Company, 1941.

——. *Songs and Stories about Animals*. Boston: Boston Music Company, 1947.

Kodály, Zoltán. *Fifty Nursery Songs*, English words by Percy M. Young. London: Boosey and Hawkes Music Publishers, 1964.

Magic of Music–K. Boston: Ginn and Company, 1965.

Making Music Your Own–K. Morristown, N.J.: Silver Burdett Company, 1971.

McCall, Adeline. *Timothy's Tunes*. Boston: Boston Music Company, 1943.

McLaughlin, Roberta, and Wood, Lucille. *The Small Singer*. Bowmar Publishing Corporation, 1969.

Raebeck, Lois. *Who Am I?* Chicago: Follett Publishing Company, 1970.

Rogers, Fred. *Mister Rogers' Song Book*. New York: Random House, 1970.

Sharing Music–K. Cincinnati: American Book Company, 1966.

3
Rhythm

RHYTHM IN MUSIC encompasses several things. One aspect of rhythm is the *pulse* or beat of the music. Pulse, the steady recurrence of accented sound, is analogous to the pulse in a human body or the ticking of a clock. The speed of the pulse may vary from song to song. In between the beats in music are varying numbers of sounds, and these patterns of sound form the actual rhythm of the music. For the purposes of this chapter, the pulse or beat will be marked by a vertical straight line over the appropriate syllable of the word.

Children from birth on show a strong feeling for rhythm. Perhaps this comes from hearing the maternal heartbeat *in utero*. Both toddlers and older children delight in feeling the rhythm of music and may spontaneously begin clapping or swaying when they hear music. Rhythm is thus an important skill to build on and should be an integral part of the music program. Clapping speech patterns, chanting, echoing, clapping and playing rhythms in songs, and listening to rhythms throughout the day are good rhythmic activities for young children.

CLAPPING SPEECH PATTERNS
Clapping and Rhythm

Clapping the simple rhythms in speech patterns is an excellent way for children to begin feeling rhythm. The concept of using speech patterns to develop rhythmic awareness in children was developed by the educator and composer Carl

Orff.[1] A good activity to begin with is clapping words. Children love to clap their own names. The teacher begins by chanting the child's name—for example:

TAPE

I-van, I-van, I-van

Each syllable of the word is then clapped. Thus a name like Ivan would have two claps, a name like Theresa would have three claps, and Sam would have just one:

TAPE

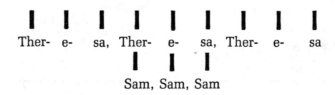

Ther- e- sa, Ther- e- sa, Ther- e- sa

Sam, Sam, Sam

The teacher should encourage the children to say the name and clap along. At first some children may clap indiscriminately, with no apparent feel for the rhythm of the name. Gradually, however, they will catch on and have a new feeling for the way words are constructed. Some children may not wish to have their names clapped, and the teacher can either skip them or ask if there is another word they would like to clap. Once children are accustomed to clapping first names, they can begin clapping first and last names:

TAPE

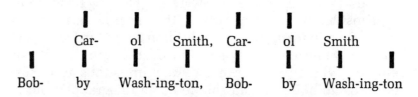

Car- ol Smith, Car- ol Smith

Bob- by Wash-ing-ton, Bob- by Wash-ing-ton

Note that in this example there are more syllables than beats. The teacher can either clap the beats, in which case there will be four claps, or the syllables, in which case there will be five claps. Later the teacher can further extend the children's rhythmic memory by stringing several names together:[2]

TAPE

Car- ol Smith (silence), Bob- by Wash-ing-ton

Names, of course, are not the only words children can clap.
They can clap animal names, flowers, foods, transportation vehicles, and so on. These rhythmic activities can be coordinated with the rest of the curriculum. For example, if the class is studying transportation, the children can clap transportation vehicles (Example 3.1).

Rhythm Instruments

Once children become skilled at clapping rhythms, they can begin playing these rhythms on rhythm instruments such as drums or sticks. These instruments are described more thoroughly in Chapter 4. The teacher should remember that an instrument on which the children play rhythms should be one that makes one clear sound per stroke (such as a drum), as opposed to an instrument such as jingle bells, where the sound is diffuse and tends to obliterate the clarity of the rhythm.

What do children learn from clapping rhythms such as these? They learn to listen carefully to the sounds they hear and to feel these sounds with their bodies. They also learn how to break words into syllables, an important prereading skill.

Example 3.1
Chant of names of transportation vehicles

| | | | | | | | |

Air-plane,   air-plane,   riv-er boat,   riv-er boat,

| | | | | | | |

Hel-i-cop-ter, hel-i-cop-ter, car (silence), car (silence),

| | | | | | | |

Rock-et ship, rock-et ship, dump truck, dump truck,

| | | | | | | |

Train (silence), train (silence), sail-boat,   sail-boat,

| | | |

Bus (silence), bus (silence).

Many two-year-old children cannot yet clap simple words such as names, but some can. At this age children may enjoy clapping so much that they do not want to slow down and listen to a pattern. Two-year-olds also may be unable to understand and follow the teacher's directions and thus may end up clapping indiscriminately. Despite the difficulty of the task, however, most children in this age group enjoy clapping activities. If the teacher continues very pronounced clapping on the syllables of the name or word, most of the children will eventually be able to imitate the rhythmic clapping successfully.

Preschool Children

Three-, four-, and five-year-olds may also have some initial difficulty with clapping words. How quickly they can master the task depends on a combination of things: their age, their developmental stage, their previous exposure to language and music, and possibly some inborn talent. Most preschool children quickly learn to clap the syllables of words and enjoy repeating this activity even after they have moved on to more difficult clapping activities.

Primary-Age Children

Primary-age children can usually clap simple words quite easily. Still, it is best for the teacher to start with this activity to make certain the children have a firm foundation for later, more complicated rhythm activities. Teachers of primary-age children can usually move on quickly to clapping combinations of words.

CHANTING
Chanting and Rhythm

Chanting is another good rhythmic activity for young children. When people chant, they recite a poem or group of words in a very accented manner, so that a pulse is apparent.

Many Mother Goose rhymes are easy to chant, and there is no question that children enjoy saying chants such as the old favorite "Peas Porridge" (Example 3.2). The problem with Mother Goose rhymes in the preschool is that although the children enjoy saying them, they have no idea what they mean. Teachers can make up much more appropriate chants that the children will enjoy saying while also understanding the meaning. In this way the teacher can gear the chant to currently relevant subject manner. "I Can Run" (Example 3.3)

44

Example 3.2
PEAS PORRIDGE

Traditional

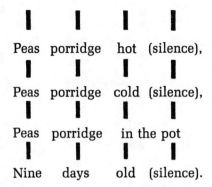

Peas porridge hot (silence),

Peas porridge cold (silence),

Peas porridge in the pot

Nine days old (silence).

is a teacher-composed chant that has the same rhythm as "Peas Porridge" but is easily understood by even very young children and is more relevant to their everyday experience.

Teachers can also use the words to preexisting songs as chants. The words to "Raining" (Example 3.4; music given in Example 2.3) make an excellent chant.

Along with saying chants, children can also clap the beats, which helps them to feel the natural pulse of the words.

Example 3.3
I CAN RUN

Sally Moomaw

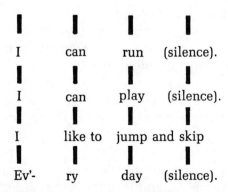

I can run (silence).

I can play (silence).

I like to jump and skip

Ev'- ry day (silence).

Example 3.4
RAINING

Ethel Crowninshield

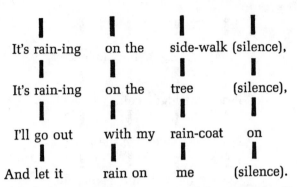

It's rain-ing	on the	side-walk	(silence),
It's rain-ing	on the	tree	(silence),
I'll go out	with my	rain-coat	on
And let it	rain on	me	(silence).

Source: Ethel Crowninshield, *New Songs and Games* (Boston: Boston Music Company, 1941). Used by permission of the copyright owner: THE BOSTON MUSIC COMPANY, Boston, MA 02216.

Later they can play the beats on rhythm instruments. At first the chants should be short and simple. Later, when the children have had sufficient practice in chanting, the chants can be longer and more complex.

Age Levels and Chants   As with songs, primary-age children can usually handle longer chants than can three- and four-year-olds, although individual children vary widely in their capabilities. Toddlers generally need very short, simple chants. This section gives examples of specific chants for specific age groups, but it is most important to remember that individual children in each age group may need more or less difficult chants. It is the teacher's responsibility to assess the needs of the children as a group and of individual children.

Toddlers   Since most toddlers have a limited command of language and relatively short memories, very short, simple. chants are desirable. Two-year-olds develop both language and memory capacity rapidly; the teacher should be alert to their quick development and introduce longer chants when appropriate.

"Who Can Play" (Example 3.5) is a very simple chant that can be used with young toddlers. "Two Shoes" (Example 3.6)

Example 3.5
WHO CAN PLAY

Sally Moomaw

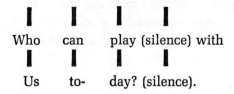

Who   can   play (silence) with

Us   to-   day? (silence).

On subsequent times, replace "Who"
with a child's name.

Example 3.6
TWO SHOES

Edna Ruff

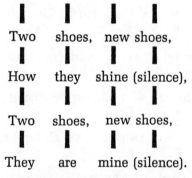

Two   shoes,   new shoes,

How   they   shine (silence),

Two   shoes,   new shoes,

They   are   mine (silence).

Source: Laura Bryant and Edna Ruff, *Still More Sentence Songs* (Cincinnati: Willis Music Company, 1945). Used by permission, Willis Music Co., Inc.

is a little longer and works well with two-and-a-half- or three-year-olds if they have first had practice with shorter chants.

Toddlers often repeat favorite words or phrases over and over, and these are good for chanting and clapping:

This   is my school (silence).

Preschool Children   "Two Shoes" (Example 3.6) is a good beginning chant for children ages three to five. Later they can say and clap longer chants. Teachers can use the words of preexisting songs or poems as chants, or they can make them up. "The Shivers" (Example 3.7) comes from the words to a song.

Children in the primary grades usually have better-developed

TAPE

Example 3.7
THE SHIVERS

Daniel Hooley

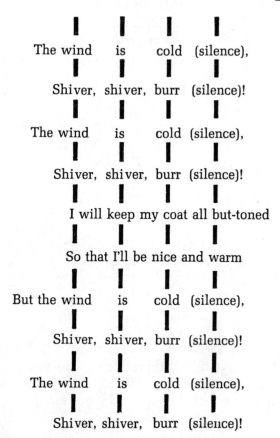

Source: From *Sharing Music*, Level K of the MUSIC FOR YOUNG AMERICANS series by Richard Berg et al., Copyright ©1966 (Cincinnati: American Book Company). Reprinted by permission of American Book Company.

memories than do preschool children and are thus capable of longer chants. The teacher should begin with a simple chant, such as "I Can Run" (Example 3.3). Once the children have mastered the concept of chanting and clapping the beats, they can try a longer, more difficult chant, "I Have a Garden" (Example 3.8)

Echoing, discussed in Chapter 2, is an excellent but rather **ECHOING** difficult rhythmic activity.[3] The teacher begins by clapping **Echoing and Rhythm** a very simple rhythm and asking the children to clap it back. As with echo songs, the children may initially want to clap along with the teacher rather than first listening to the rhythm. Also, when they begin to echo the clapping, the group may have a difficult time staying together. The resulting echo may sound like a swarm of locusts. The teacher

Example 3.8
I HAVE A GARDEN

Sally Moomaw

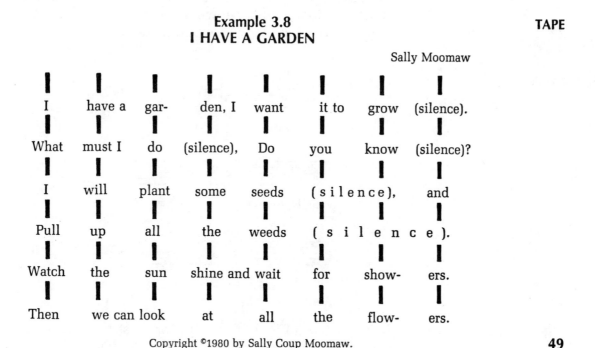

can overcome these problems by having an assistant or parent lead the echo group, or by having the children echo individually. It is important to remember that this is a difficult skill that the children may need time to learn. Echoing should not be started until the children are already accustomed to clapping rhythms in words or chants.

If a group of children becomes very adept at echoing, the teacher may wish to introduce *drum talking*, where the teacher plays something on the drum and the child plays it back. Alternatively, the teacher may ask a child to play something on the drum and then play it back to the child.

Beginning echoes should be very short:

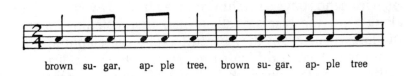

brown su- gar,   ap- ple tree,   brown su- gar,   ap- ple tree

A teacher who cannot read rhythms can generate rhythms by thinking of words or simple phrases and then clapping them. Thinking of the verbal cues in the foregoing example will produce the rhythms shown. Later, echoes can be made longer by stringing several rhythm patterns together:

TAPE

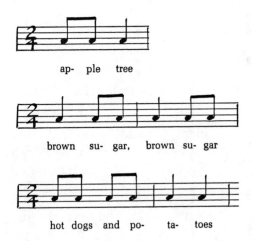

ap- ple   tree

brown   su- gar,   brown su- gar

hot dogs and po-   ta-   toes

Age Levels and Echoing

Echoing is too difficult a concept for most two-year-olds. Three- and four-year-olds also have difficulty echoing but can acquire the skill with experience. Primary-age children are usually cognitively well equipped for echoing, but individual children may understand the concept but not yet have the perception required to remember and repeat a pattern. Primary-age children usually enjoy the game aspect and the challenge of echoing.

RHYTHM IN SONGS

Children can become more aware of the rhythm of songs by clapping as they sing. If the teacher begins clapping the beat, the children will soon join in. Not every song should be clapped since this may distract the children from hearing other things in the music, but clapping songs occasionally is a good way to emphasize rhythm.

The teacher may also occasionally suggest that instead of singing a song, the class say and clap the words. In this way they will be clapping the actual rhythm of the song, rather than just the beat.

Playing rhythm instruments along with songs is another good way to emphasize rhythm. This is discussed fully in Chapter 4.

RHYTHM THROUGHOUT THE DAY

Rhythm should be an important part of the classroom, not just a once-a-day activity at music time. Children explore rhythms all day long as they play, and the teacher should use these opportunities to explore rhythm with them. The sound of rain hitting the roof has a rhythm they can listen to. The ticking of a clock has another. On the playground the teacher can point out such things as the sound a ball makes as it bounces, or the squeak of the teeter-totter.

Children often chant spontaneously. They love the sounds that words make and say certain phrases over and over. The teacher can show that he or she values this by chanting along with them. The teacher can also introduce chants at appropriate times during the day.

SUMMARY

Children gain important listening skills as well as much enjoyment from working with rhythms. The teacher should include at least one rhythmic activity in each music group. Clapping names or words and clapping along with songs are good beginning rhythmic activities. Later, chanting poems and echoing can be added. The teacher can gain important ideas about rhythms to use with the class by listening to the words the children chant as they play and emphasizing the rhythms they hear throughout the day.

NOTES

1. Some of Orff's examples can be found in Carl Orff and Gunild Keetman, *Music for Children*, English version by Margaret Murray (London: Schott and Company, 1958), p. 50.

2. In this and the following examples, the word *silence* will be used to indicate natural rests in the flow of the words.

3. See Orff and Keetman, *Music for Children*, pp. 53–55, for some fairly elaborate examples of echoing.

SELECTED BIBLIOGRAPHY

Findlay, Elsa. *Rhythm and Movement: Applications of Dalcroze Eurhythmics*. Evanston, Ill.: Summy-Birchard Company, 1971.

Orff, Carl, and Keetman, Gunild. *Music for Children*, Vol. 1, English version by Margaret Murray. London: Schott and Company, 1958.

Weissman, Jackie. *Miss Jackie Says: Hello Rhythm*. Library of Congress Catalog #77-81971, 1977.

4

Instruments

USING INSTRUMENTS opens a whole new dimension in the understanding of sound and the awareness of music in young children. Through experimenting with instruments, children acquire important concepts about the nature of sound and how sound is affected by the instrument itself and the manner in which it is played. Instruments also give children an excellent means for expressing their feelings and provide a ready medium for their burgeoning creativity. Moreover, playing musical instruments helps children develop their eye-hand coordination and fine motor skills.

Three different types of instruments may be used successfully with young children: rhythm instruments, melody instruments, and accompanying instruments. *Rhythm instruments* are those that, when struck or scraped, produce a variety of nonpitched sounds. *Melody instruments* produce sounds with specific pitches so that tunes or melodies can be played on them. Finally, *accompanying instruments* produce several tones simultaneously, thus creating chords that may be used to accompany melodies.

RHYTHM INSTRUMENTS

There are a number of rhythm instruments that are often used with young children. Adults may think of these instruments as toys, but they are real musical instruments; most of them are found in the percussion sections of symphony orchestras. Although children need some leeway to experiment with percussion instruments, they should also be taught to respect them as legitimate musical instruments and to treat them appropriately.

Types of Rhythm Instruments
Tone Blocks or Wood Blocks

Tone blocks are hollowed-out wooden blocks that produce a resonant tone when struck with a small wooden beater or mallet. Some are rectangular, others cylindrical with a handle. Children may wish to experiment by striking them with different types of material and observing how this alters the tone.

Rhythm Sticks

Rhythm sticks are perhaps the most commonly used rhythm instrument. They are a pair of wooden sticks that are played by holding one still and striking it with the other. Some rhythm sticks are smooth and some are serrated. The latter type can also be played by scraping one stick along the ridges of the other.

Claves

Claves (pronounced CLAH-vays) are very similar to rhythm sticks but are shorter and wider. One clave is held in the cupped palm of the hand, so that the hand helps it to resonate. It is struck with the other clave.

Guiros (pronounced GWEAR-rose) are hollowed-out gourds with ridges carved into them. They are played by scraping a stick across the ridges.

Guiros

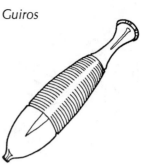

Triangles are metal rods bent into a triangular shape and played with a metal striker. In order to vibrate and thus sound properly, the triangle must be suspended from a triangle holder. When played correctly, the triangle is struck on the side opposite the opening. This distinction is probably not particularly important to young children; however, they may wish to experiment by striking the triangle with metal, wood, and rubber and noting the different sound each makes. Triangles are sometimes difficult for young children to play; they tend to twist on the holder, and hitting a moving target is difficult. Some triangles have straight metal sticks for holders, which prevent the triangle from twisting and thus make it easier to play. Triangles are usually quite popular with young children, perhaps because they produce such a lovely, ringing sound.

Triangles

Cymbals are a pair of concave metal disks with handles. To achieve the best tone quality, the cymbals are held parallel to each other and tilted slightly; the bottom cymbal is held still while the top cymbal strikes the stationary cymbal with an arc-shaped motion. Usually the motion is downward, but successive strokes may be alternated down-up. Some children's cymbals make a very unpleasant sound; others, usually more expensive, have a lovely ring. It is well worth buying the more expensive pair since their sound much more nearly approaches that of regular cymbals, and their aesthetically pleasing tone encourages children to regard them as musical instruments rather than noisemakers. This is an important consideration in helping children develop discriminating ears.

Cymbals

Finger Cymbals

Finger cymbals are much smaller than regular cymbals—about two inches in diameter. They make a lovely, tinkling sound when played by holding one horizontally and striking the edge with the edge of the other cymbal.

Maracas

Maracas are hollowed-out gourds filled with seeds. They have handles and are shaken like rattles. Maracas break easily if they are hit against the floor or other hard objects.

Castanets

Castanets are a pair of wooden disks, usually joined together at one edge with elastic. They are held in one hand and clicked together. Castanets are more difficult for children to play than are most of the other rhythm instruments because holding them and playing them requires a great deal of finger strength and fine-motor control. Some castanets, however, are mounted on wood and played by tapping them against the wood. These are easier to play since they do not require the fine degree of coordination necessary with regular castanets.

Tambourines

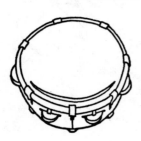

Tambourines are circular frames of wood with a plastic or skin head stretched over one side and jingles mounted on the frame. They are played by striking the head with the knuckles or tapping it with the fingers. They can also be shaken so that only the jingles sound.

Drums are cylinders of wood or plastic with skin or plastic heads stretched over either one or both ends. They can be played with either the hand or a mallet (beater). Some drums can be tuned to a specific pitch by tightening or loosening the head; others have no specific pitch. Some drums, called *snare drums*, have metal or gut strips under the drumhead that produce a rattling sound when the drum is struck.

Drums should be played approximately midway between the center of the drum and the rim. When they are struck in the center of the drumhead, a dull "thunk" is produced.

Drums vary greatly in both quality and price. Those classified as Latin American drums are better made and more resonant than are the inexpensive drums with handles. The Orff-type drums with tunable heads are by far the most resonant drums. Drums with rubber heads do not resonate well, and the heads break easily.

Drums

Jingle bells or sleigh bells are small bells mounted on wooden handles or bracelets of elastic.

Jingle Bells

Jingle sticks are small wooden frames with metal jingles, like those found on tambourines, mounted on them. They can be shaken or tapped against the palm of the hand that is not holding them.

Jingle Sticks

Cowbells Cowbells are metal bells that are struck with a beater. They produce a loud, clunky sound. Nevertheless, they are a legitimate part of the percussion section of the orchestra.

Sand Blocks Sand blocks are blocks of wood covered on one side with sandpaper. The sandpaper sides of the blocks are rubbed together to produce a scraping sound.

Selecting Rhythm Instruments The list of rhythm instruments is so long that it may seem mind-boggling. Although each instrument has merit in that it produces a distinctive sound, it is not necessary to buy every instrument on the list. It is important, however, to have several types of instruments so that children can observe that different instruments are played in different ways and have different sounds.

Tone blocks, rhythm sticks, and claves all make similar sounds; it might be wise to select one of these instruments rather than buying all three. All these instruments are excellent for developing the rhythm skills discussed in Chapter 3, because they make one clear sound per stroke and are easy to play. Tone blocks have an advantage over sticks in that they are smaller; the energetic child is less likely to hit his or her neighbor inadvertently while playing a tone block than while playing the sticks. It is advisable to have at least four or five tone blocks for preschool classes so that if the instruments are used in a group experience, no child will have to wait too long for a turn. Primary classes need even more wood blocks since there are usually more children per class. Fortunately, these instruments are inexpensive.

Triangles are very popular and should also be included

in a class's instrument inventory. Their single metallic sound contrasts nicely with the wooden sound produced by the wood blocks or sticks. Thus triangles can be used very effectively to help young children develop auditory discrimination.

Drums, tambourines, and jingle bells are also popular with young children. All three are good instruments to use for accompanying songs.

Tone blocks, sticks, claves, triangles, and jingle bells are all relatively inexpensive and durable. Drums, tambourines, and maracas are more expensive and less durable. If the children are supervised while playing these latter instruments, however, they, too, should last.

Introducing Rhythm Instruments

If children are to develop good auditory discrimination, instruments need to be presented singly rather than all at once. When teachers hand out a variety of rhythm instruments to be played simultaneously, as often happens, the children are unable to distinguish the sound of each individual instrument. Moreover, the resulting noise does not permit the children to hear the music or follow the rhythm. Therefore, teachers should begin by giving the children one type of instrument for the first several sessions. Then, when the children clearly recognize the sound this instrument makes, the teacher can introduce a second type. More instruments can be added gradually, but always one type of instrument at a time. The teacher will need to continue reviewing with the children the instruments they already know. Eventually the children will learn to identify the sound of each instrument.

The introduction of rhythm instruments might follow a pattern similar to this:

First Day

The teacher shows the children a wood block and plays it while they listen. The teacher and children talk about the sound the wood block makes. Then the teacher hands out several wood blocks and invites the children to play them. The wood blocks are passed around until every child has had a chance to try them. The teacher collects the wood blocks and moves on to another activity, but leaves several wood blocks out in the room so that children who are interested can have more opportunity to play them.

Second Day   The teacher again shows the children a wood block and asks if they remember what it is called or what it sounds like. The teacher again plays the instrument for the children. Next, the teacher explains that the children can use the wood blocks to play some rhythms. The teacher and children say and clap a familiar chant, such as "Rain, Rain, Go Away" (Example 4.1). Then several children play wood blocks while the rest of the class says and claps the chant. (Some children will play the wood blocks on the beat, and some will not.) The chant is repeated until all those children who are interested have had an opportunity to play the wood blocks. The teacher reminds the children that some of the wood blocks will be left out in the room if anyone would like to use them again.

Third Day   The teacher and children repeat the activities of the second day.

Fourth Day   The teacher shows the children the wood block and then introduces a new instrument, the triangle. The children talk about how the triangle looks, sounds, and feels, and what it is made of. Then the teacher plays the wood block and the triangle, one right after the other. The children talk about the difference in the sound of the two instruments and how the sound is produced. Next, the teacher passes out several triangles for the children to try. The triangles are passed around until every child has had a chance to play a triangle. The teacher leaves several triangles out in the room for interested children to play later.

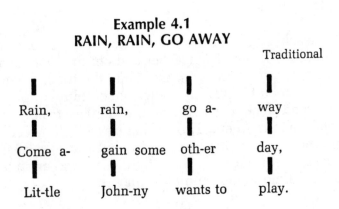

Example 4.1
RAIN, RAIN, GO AWAY

Traditional

Rain,	rain,	go a-	way
Come a-	gain some	oth-er	day,
Lit-tle	John-ny	wants to	play.

60

The teacher again shows the wood block and triangle, and the sound is again compared. The children then say and chant "Rain, Rain, Go Away," after which they play it on triangles. The teacher leaves several triangles and wood blocks out so that the children can compare the sounds.

Fifth Day

Individual instruments are introduced in the same way, always one at a time, and each is compared with the instruments the children already know. Although later they will be used to accompany songs, initially they are played with nonmelodic rhythm activities so that the sound of the instruments is not obscured. The instruments are left out in the room for supervised experimentation.

Subsequent Days

Contrast this planned introduction of instruments with the so-called rhythm band, in which various instruments are passed out and played simultaneously. The resulting noise does not allow the children to distinguish the sound of any one instrument or to hear the music, much less try to play on the beat. The rhythm band activity does not enable the children to form concepts about sound, learn to identify instruments, gain a feeling for rhythm, or hear the music.

Rhythm instruments are a delight to infants. Even before they are old enough to grasp objects, they can watch and listen intently while an adult plays these instruments for them. Later, when they are old enough to hold objects, they can begin to make sounds with the instruments that shake. Maracas (if they are small enough for an infant to hold) and jingle bells are appropriate for this age. (The jingle bells should be inspected carefully before they are given to the baby to make sure that the bells are firmly attached and cannot be worked loose and swallowed.) Still later, infants reach a stage where they begin to use one object to strike another. At this point they really begin to enjoy drums (and pans!). A triangle can be suspended so that the infant can strike it and make a sound. This requires well-developed eye-hand coordination, and practicing this kind of activity helps the child develop fine motor ability. (Triangle strikers can be dangerous at this age, since a baby might fall with the striker in his or her mouth. Children this young must be supervised by an adult at all times when holding sticks.) Bells and tone

Activities with Rhythm Instruments
Infants

blocks can also be suspended so that infants can experiment with the different sounds these materials make.

If an adult sings while an infant is playing a rhythm instrument, the infant begins to get a feel for sound accompanying sound. Infants also enjoy playing their instrument along with a record. Participating in the music-making process is important even for very young children.

Toddlers

Toddlers continue to experiment with the sounds instruments make. Since toddlers are larger and stronger than infants, they can play some of the larger rhythm instruments, such as tambourines, standard-size maracas, and cymbals. Their coordination has also progressed, so older toddlers can play those instruments that must be held in one hand and played with the other—triangles, sticks, and tone blocks.

Toddlers can begin to use rhythm instruments to accompany the songs they know. Instruments that are shaken, such as maracas and bells, are the easiest ones for them to play as they listen or sing. If toddlers are participating in any kind of group experience, however informal it may be, it is good to have an instrument for each child since toddlers have greater difficulty waiting for turns than preschoolers.

"Hear Our Jingle Bells" (Example 4.2) is an easy song for toddlers to accompany with bells. The tune and words are simple, and the song can be sung over and over again, using a different child's name each time. Adults may tire of the song much sooner than the children do! Most toddlers will ring the bells indiscriminately without regard for rhythm, but an observant adult may notice a few already beginning to play on the beat.

TAPE

Example 4.2
HEAR OUR JINGLE BELLS

Sally Moomaw

Jin- gle jin- gle   jin- gle,   Hear our jin- gle   bells.
Jin- gle jin- gle   jin- gle,   Dan- ny plays his   bells.

Copyright ©1979, 1980 by Sally Coup Moomaw.

Three-, four-, and five-year-olds continue to experiment with sound, and rhythm instruments provide a good medium for such experimentation. In addition, preschool children can use rhythm instruments to accompany and enhance familiar songs. The instruments can be used to play the beat of the music or to express the mood of the song. For example, in "Hammering" (Example 2.25) the children can play drums on the beat and thus emphasize the rhythm while recreating the sound of the hammers. The children should first sing the song, then clap on the beats while they sing, and finally add the drums on the beats. If the drums are handed out before the children clap the beats, they are likely to be so excited about playing the drums that they forget to listen for the pulse of the music; therefore, clap the beat and sing before passing out the instruments.

Some children do not have a feel for the beat in music. This skill develops much later in some children than in others. The teacher should not draw attention to the child who seems to be playing the drum or clapping indiscriminately. A feel for the pulse of the music will develop gradually, although it may take years for certain children to develop this skill.

When rhythm instruments are used to accompany songs, they need not be relegated just to playing the beat. Some songs are greatly enhanced when a specific instrument is used only in certain parts of the song. Children who are four and older may enjoy saving their instruments for particular parts of the song, whereas younger children may have more difficulty waiting to play the instruments. As an example, the song "Thunder" (Example 2.4) can be augmented by cymbal crashes, suggesting the sound of thunder, on the words of longer duration at the end of each line.

Similarly, "Rain, Snow, and Hail" (Example 4.3) can be accompanied by a triangle on the words "plink, plunk"; by sand blocks on the words "swish, swish"; and by cymbals on the words "crash, clump."

Still another use of rhythm instruments is to accompany movements. The teacher can select instruments with different sounds to evoke different moods. For example, a steady beat on a drum might be used to accompany children walking like bears; a light tinkling on finger cymbals or a triangle might be used to stimulate the children to dramatize scurrying mice.

Example 4.3
RAIN, SNOW, AND HAIL

Sally Moomaw

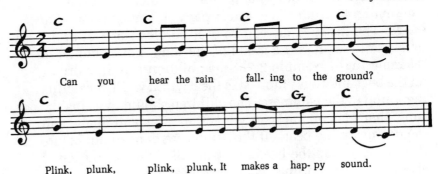

Can you hear the rain fall-ing to the ground?

Plink, plunk, plink, plunk, It makes a hap-py sound.

2. Can you hear the snow falling to the ground?
Swish, swish, swish, swish, It hardly makes a sound!

3. Can you hear the hail falling to the ground?
Crash, clump, crash, clump, It makes a noisy sound!

The teacher might play something on an instrument and ask the children to dramatize what the sounds remind them of, or a child could play something on a rhythm instrument for other children to act out.

Primary-Age Children First-, second-, and third-grade children also enjoy accompanying songs with rhythm instruments. Once they have become skillful at accompanying their singing with one instrument, they can begin to combine two different instruments playing two different rhythmic patterns in a song. This type of activity is discussed in detail in Chapter 8 ("Orff Concepts with Young Children").

When introducing rhythm instruments with primary-age children, the same sequence should be followed as with preschoolers. They should be presented one instrument at a time, with enough time allowed for the children to learn the sound of each instrument before another is introduced.

MELODY INSTRUMENTS Melody instruments, as the name implies, are those with an assortment of pitches so that melodies can be played on them.

The melody instruments most commonly used with young children are the xylophone, the melody bells, and the zither.

The xylophone consists of a series of wooden bars graduated in length to sound the musical scale. It is mounted on a frame, usually of wood, and is played by striking the bars with a mallet. A variety of mallets are available—wood, hard rubber, yarn, and felt—each with its own characteristic sound. *Glockenspiels* are similar to xylophones but have metal bars rather than wood. They can be used in the same way as xylophones. Xylophones and glockenspiels come in an assortment of sizes, which correspond to how high and low they play. Xylophones are sized soprano (high); alto (medium); and bass (low, pronounced BASE). Glockenspiels come in two sizes, soprano and alto.

Types of Melody Instruments
Xylophone

There are many inexpensive toy xylophones on the market. They usually have metal bars and thus resemble glockenspiels. Their tone quality is greatly inferior to the more expensive xylophones. In addition, good xylophones have removable bars; activities that involve using only selected bars of the xylophone are discussed in Chapter 8.

Melody bells or resonator bells are metal bars of varying length mounted on wooden blocks and arranged like a piano keyboard. They are also played with a mallet, and the individual bells can be removed from the set.

Melody Bells

A zither consists of a frame with strings of graduated length that are plucked with the finger or a pick.

Zither

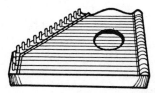

Selecting Melody Instruments

The most versatile melody instruments are the high-quality xylophones and glockenspiels. These instruments have removable bars that allow them to be tuned to major, minor, and pentatonic scales. (See Chapter 8 and the Glossary concerning these scales.) Their sound is beautiful, and, when treated appropriately, they are extremely durable.

Good-quality xylophones and glockenspiels are considerably more expensive than their toy counterparts; unlike toy xylophones, however, they are real musical instruments scaled down to child size. Toy xylophones have very little use in the classroom, but removable-bar melody instruments are extremely versatile and can be used for a wealth of musical activities. Chapter 8 discusses how children can use these instruments to compose melodies, play accompaniments, and even create *polyphony* (pronounced po-LIH-foe-nee): two or more melodies playing simultaneously.

Buying a good instrument is like buying any other high-quality material for the classroom. Though more expensive, they are instruments of quality and durability. Many activities require the use of just one instrument, so it is entirely feasible to start with one instrument and add another each year. The alto xylophone is an excellent choice for a first instrument. Its larger size makes it easier to play than the glockenspiels. Next an alto glockenspiel might be selected so that children can compare the timbre of the wooden xylophone with that of the metallic glockenspiel. Later a soprano xylophone and glockenspiel might be added, or even a metallophone. *Metallophones* are similar in size to xylophones but have metal bars that continue to vibrate for a period of time after they are struck.

Using Melody Instruments with Children

Infants and Toddlers

Late infancy or toddlerhood is a good time to introduce the xylophone, since children of this age are eagerly experimenting with hitting one object against another. The xylophone, with its pleasing sound, is thus of great interest to children of this age. Through continued experimentation, the toddler can begin to formulate some concepts of the nature of pitch.

Preschool Children

Children who are three, four, and five years old can play all three melody instruments—xylophone, melody bells, and zither. Some children play these instruments just to listen to the sounds they make, and the teacher can help them listen carefully to the difference in the sounds made by the different lengths of bar (the shorter the bar, the higher the pitch) and the different types of mallet. They can also be encouraged to watch and feel the vibrating strings on the zither. In addition to listening carefully to the sounds they produce on the instruments, children might be encouraged to try to sing the pitch of the note they are playing. The teacher might introduce the terms *high* and *low* for the sounds produced by the long and short bars (see Chapter 7 on musical concepts). Some children may try to recreate familiar melodies or make up songs of their own. The teacher can encourage such creativity by singing back the child's tune or recording it on a cassette.

Zithers have a pleasant sound but are more difficult for young children to play than are xylophones or melody bells because better coordination is needed to pluck the appropriate string. If children are playing the zither with their fingers, keep a close watch for blisters, which can develop quickly.

Children in the early grades also enjoy xylophones and zithers. In addition, melody bells are commonly used in primary schools. Children can compose tunes on bells, and some children in this age group can learn to play simple songs such as "Mary Had a Little Lamb." Children can also use resonator bells to play simple patterns to accompany songs, as discussed in Chapter 8.

Primary-Age Children

Three instruments are often used to accompany songs with children: the piano, the autoharp, and the guitar. The piano is more common in primary schools than in nursery schools. Although it is an excellent accompanying instrument, it has two serious drawbacks. First, it takes several years of training for a person to acquire sufficient technique to accompany songs; second, the piano itself is so large that it imposes a considerable physical barrier between the teacher and the children. The autoharp and guitar are more easily played and, since they are small, can be held on the lap, with the performer seated on the floor and the children gathered around. This fosters a more intimate relationship between teacher and children. Finally, autoharps and guitars are portable and can be taken outdoors or wherever the children are.

ACCOMPANYING INSTRUMENTS

Autoharp

The autoharp is an ideal instrument for teachers because they need no musical training in order to play it. The music to many songs includes autoharp chords, notated as letters above the music that correspond to the chords on the autoharp.

There are two ways to hold the autoharp. Folk singers hold it vertically on the lap in order to use a variety of picking patterns. The autoharp can also be held flat on the lap. The latter may be a preferable position for teachers of young children since this is the way children must hold the autoharp in order to play it. The left hand is used to press the button on the autoharp whose letter corresponds to the letter in the music, and the right hand is used to strum the strings. The strings are strummed with a pick on the left side of the bars, and thus the hands are crossed when the autoharp is held flat on the lap. The strings are strummed from bottom to top (longest to shortest).[1] Figure 4.1 shows the bars of the autoharp.

Since autoharps go out of tune periodically, the teacher will need a pitch pipe to help in the tuning of the instrument. Pitch pipes are usually circular with a series of holes clearly labeled to correspond to the autoharp strings. The teacher blows the desired pitch and turns the peg of the corresponding string with a tuning hammer until the sounds match. The children may want to help the teacher listen for the pitch of the string that matches the pitch pipe.

Children can play the autoharp, too. A rubber spatula

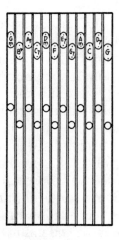

Figure 4.1 Bars of the Autoharp

makes a good strumming device that is easier for them to hold than a pick. Children begin by experimenting with pressing buttons and strumming. Then they can try a simple song that requires only one chord for the accompaniment. In "Wind Song" (Example 4.4) the capital Fs above the music indicate that F is the chord to be played on the autoharp.

Later, interested children can begin accompanying songs with two chords. This is excellent training in auditory discrimination because they can begin to distinguish the sounds of different chords. "Here We Go Round the Mulberry Bush" (Example 2.21) is a song with two chords.

There is also a child-size version of the autoharp on the market. It has only five chords, but it can be used for many of the simple accompaniments that children can play.

Guitar

The guitar is also a suitable accompanying instrument and, like the autoharp, is readily portable. The guitar is harder to learn to play than the autoharp, but learning the relatively small number of chords necessary to accompany most songs should not be too difficult. Preschool and primary-age children cannot play the guitar because their fingers are not long enough to reach the chords.

MAKING INSTRUMENTS
Common Self-Made Instruments

Making instruments is an excellent way for children to learn more about the properties of sound, as well as an economical way to supply instruments for the class. If children are to develop discriminating ears and some feeling for the quality of a musical instrument, however, care must be used in

Example 4.4
WIND SONG

Original key: G   Laura Bryant

Blow,   blow.   March wind,   blow.
Go,   go,   win- ter   snow.

Source: Laura Bryant and Edna Ruff, *Still More Sentence Songs* (Cincinnati: Willis Music Company, 1945). Used by permission, Willis Music Co., Inc.

selecting child-made or teacher-made instruments that will have an acceptable sound.

Maracas

One of the easiest instruments to make is a maraca. It can be made from a film container, a dried gourd, a covered can, or various other materials. It can be filled with rice, popcorn, or some other similar substance. All these materials seem to make maracas that sound acceptable. Rather than telling the children how to make the maraca, the teacher can make available a variety of containers and fillers and let the children experiment with how the various combinations sound. Such concrete experimentation with sound devices helps the children formulate concepts about the nature of sound.

Sand Blocks

Sand blocks are also easy to construct by stapling or gluing sandpaper onto blocks of wood or even unit blocks. The teacher might let the children experiment with different grades of sandpaper to see how they affect the sound. Also, various sizes of wood can be used since the size of the wood affects how high or low the sand block will sound.

Water Glasses

A simple musical scale can be constructed by filling water glasses to varying depths. The glasses must all be of the same size and thickness. The higher the water level in the glass, the lower the pitch. The children can experiment with water levels and hear how this alters the pitch. Simple tunes can be played on the glasses.

Coconut Shells

Another resonant instrument that teachers can make is a hollowed-out coconut shell. Coconut shells are often used to depict the sound of galloping horses. First a hole must be drilled in the shell and the milk drained. Next the shell is cut in half and the meat scraped out. Then the shell halves should be allowed to dry. The shells can be tapped together or played with a wooden beater.

Jingle Bells

Jingle bells can also be constructed easily, although they are relatively inexpensive to buy. The bells can be purchased and fastened securely to elastic bands or ribbon.

Rhythm Sticks

Children may enjoy experimenting with making rhythm sticks out of wooden dowels. The teacher can help the children saw the dowels to the desired length. If dowels of various diameters are selected, the children can experiment with the different sounds created by the various widths.

Ethnic or Exotic Self-Made Instruments

More and more composers and percussionists are experimenting with a variety of ethnic, found, or other self-made instruments. These instruments expand the repertoire of beautiful and interesting sounds that can be used to enhance music. Many of these instruments are constructed from common household items or materials that can be obtained easily and inexpensively from a hardware store. In addition, most of the instruments are simple to build with the use of only a hammer, a saw, and a drill. The following instruments are part of the collection of Professor Allen Otte of *The Percussion Group*, College–Conservatory of Music, University of Cincinnati.

Suspended Water Cans

Suspended water cans (Figure 4.2) are constructed from cans that have lids or can be sealed, such as paint cans. A small amount of water is added to each can before the lid is replaced. The cans are then suspended by rubber bands from hooks attached to a board or wooden frame. Two rubber bands are used to support each can. The cans give a lovely ring when struck with a mallet, and the water creates an interesting *glissando* effect; that is, the pitch gradually slides up or down.

Children can explore the sound effect created by the water by experimenting with empty cans and cans with varying amounts of water. In addition, constructing this instrument

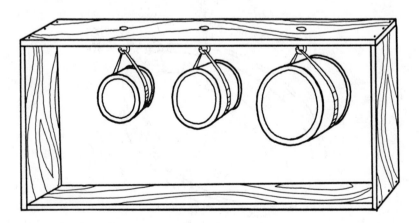

Figure 4.2 Suspended Water Cans

71

with cans of various sizes lets children experience the effect of the size of the can on pitch. Children may wish to select this instrument to accompany certain songs, such as space songs or water songs. They may also wish to use this instrument in combination with other instruments to create their own musical compositions.

Garbage Can Lid Gong

Metal garbage can lids can be used to make resonant gongs (Figure 4.3). First the handle on the garbage can is removed. Then two holes are drilled several inches apart along the rim. A small length of rope is threaded through the holes and knotted at the back of each hole to form a handle. The gong is held off the floor and struck with a mallet. Striking the lid hard produces a "splash" effect; hitting it gently creates a soft, pretty tone. Garbage can lids of various sizes can be used since each size has its own characteristic pitch. Metal wash tubs and garbage cans also make gongs with very deep, resonant tones.

Gongs are exquisite for creating special effects to highlight the climax of a song, chant, or instrumental piece. Such use of the instrument helps children gain a feel for the use of instruments to create mood in music. The children may have ideas about different ways to play the instrument to highlight various parts of the music.

Adapted Fishing Pole

To construct an adapted fishing pole, a cane fishing pole is cut at each joint in the cane. The poles are suspended above

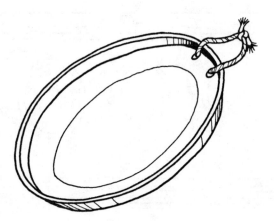

Figure 4.3   Garbage Can Lid Gong

a board approximately six to eight inches wide and as long as necessary to accommodate all the lengths of cane lying side by side. Nails are hammered partway in along the long sides of the board at about five-inch intervals. The cane poles are then suspended by twisting rubber bands around each pole and attaching the rubber bands to the nails. Several poles can be held by each rubber band, and each pole is suspended at both ends so that it hangs parallel to the board. The completed instrument resembles a xylophone (See Figure 4.4).

This instrument is a randomly pitched xylophone. In other words, the bars have specific pitches but do not conform to a traditional scale. Since each cane fishing pole will have joints of different lengths, no two instruments will sound exactly alike; hence the pitch is termed *random*. The instrument can be played by striking the individual bars or by strumming the bars quickly in one sweep to produce an interesting glissando effect.

Dowel Harp

The dowel harp (Figure 4.5) is made from half-inch dowels of varying lengths mounted on a board. Children may wish to measure lengths of dowel and saw them. Half-inch holes are drilled in a row approximately every two inches along the center of a board. The dowels are then seriated by length and glued into the holes. Striking each individual dowel does not produce a resonant sound; however, playing each dowel rapidly in succession by means of a horizontal stroke creates a sound like that of a giant guiro.

Brake Drums

Some contemporary compositions use brake drums for special effects. Discarded brake drums, which can be obtained from junkyards, produce a ringing tone when set on a table or the

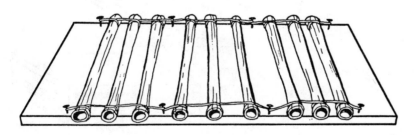

Figure 4.4 Adapted Fishing Pole

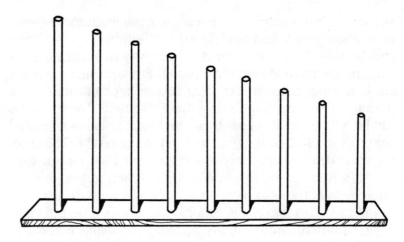

Figure 4.5   Dowel Harp

floor and struck with a mallet. Since there is some variation in the sizes of brake drums, a limited pitch variety can be obtained.

Wood Block   Resonant wood blocks can be built easily with pieces of two-by-fours and quarter-inch plywood. The two-by-four is first cut into blocks of wood, which can be of various lengths to produce different sounds. Next three small strips of plywood, each about half an inch wide, are glued to the top of the wood along both short sides and one long side. Finally, a top of

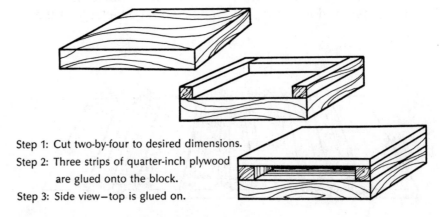

Step 1: Cut two-by-four to desired dimensions.
Step 2: Three strips of quarter-inch plywood
        are glued onto the block.
Step 3: Side view—top is glued on.

Figure 4.6   Self-Made Wood Block

quarter-inch plywood, the same size as the bottom, is glued on and held in place until dry with a clamp or weight. Children can construct their own wood blocks (See Figure 4.6) and will be amazed at the difference in sound between the glued wood block and a plain piece of two-by-four.

The alumiphone (Figure 4.7) is a beautiful and exotic instrument. It is made from lengths of one-inch aluminum pipe cut so that the pitches of adjacent pipes are much closer together than are the pitches of two adjacent keys on the piano (such tuning is called *microtonal*).[2] This is done by cutting the pipe so that each pipe is a fraction of an inch shorter than the previous pipe. The cut edges should be filed so that they are smooth. Holes are drilled 22 percent of the way down on each end of each pipe so that a cord can pass through the pipes.[3] Next the pipes are laid side by side from longest to shortest, with about half an inch of space between each two pipes, and a board is selected that is wide enough to accommodate all the pipes suspended above it. Two-inch eyelets are screwed into the board in between each pipe. A piece of plastic tubing is placed over each eyelet so that the aluminum pipes will not rattle against the eyelets. Finally, the pipes are suspended by means of a cord that passes through each pipe and eyelet.

    The alumiphone can be played by striking each individual bar or by playing all the bars with a horizontal stroke. Its lovely sound and inexpensive construction cost make it well worth the time required to build it.

Children can create interesting sound effects by playing a variety of cans of different sizes set on a table or on the floor.

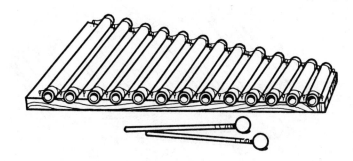

Figure 4.7 Alumiphone

Each size can will have its own pitch. Experimenting with the sounds cans make helps children formulate concepts about how the size of an instrument affects its pitch. The edges of the can where the lid was removed should be filed or taped so that the children do not cut their fingers.

Microtonal Xylophone

An exotic-sounding xylophone can be constructed in a way similar to the construction of the alumiphone by cutting hard-wood bars (rosewood, oak, maple, and the like) so that each bar is slightly shorter than the one next to it (See Figure 4.8). The bars can be suspended over a board by twisting string or cord around the ends of each bar and tying the cord to nails hammered into the wood.

Two-by-Four Marimba

An interesting marimba (See Figure 4.9) can be constructed using varying lengths of hardwood two-by-fours.[4] The wood is first cut to various lengths—18 to 20 inches might be a good length to start with. Next an area is hollowed out in the center, the width of the board, about 3.5 inches long, and 1 inch deep. The bar is held at one end and struck with a mallet. The children can compare the sound of the marimba bar to the sound of a two-by-four that has not been hollowed out. The marimba bar has a much more resonant sound and a lower pitch. Using varying lengths of bar produces different pitches, which can be tuned to a scale if desired.

Thunder Sheet

Orchestras and symphonic bands occasionally use an instrument called a thunder sheet for special effects. Thunder sheets can be easily made from pieces of galvanized sheet metal ob-

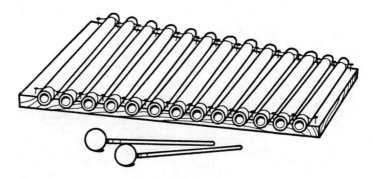

76   **Figure 4.8 Microtonal Xylophone**

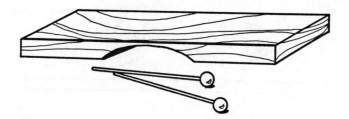

Figure 4.9 Side View of Marimba Bar

tained from sheet metal or plumbing distributors (see Figure 4.10). Thunder sheets with different sounds can be constructed by using sheets of varying sizes. Two holes are drilled at the top of the piece of sheet metal. A short length of rope is threaded through the holes and knotted at each end to form a handle. When the thunder sheet is held off the floor and struck with a mallet or shaken, it produces a sound very similar to that of thunder. An instrument like this, so inexpensive and easy to construct, is exciting for children to use to accompany songs such as "Thunder" (Example 2.4). Encouraging children to decide which instruments to use to accompany a song helps them understand how composers use sound to convey a particular feeling, mood, or idea.

Clock Coils

An interesting instrument (Figure 4.11) can be made by mounting the coils from a discarded clock onto a hollow wooden box. When the coils are struck with a beater, they produce a beautiful chime.

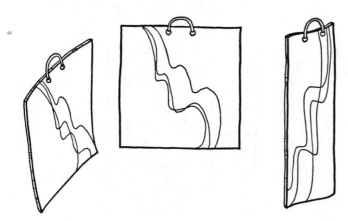

Figure 4.10 Thunder Sheets

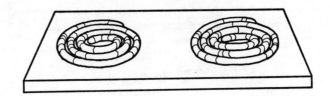

Figure 4.11   Clock Coils

Hollow Box   The instrument shown in Figure 4.12 is a five-sided hollow wooden box constructed so that each side produces a different sound. The top of the box is made from quarter-inch plywood. The length and width can vary, but eight to ten inches seems to be a good size to begin with. The sides are made of thicker wood, each the same width but of different lengths. The box is then glued together. Because of the varying dimensions of the sides and top of the box, each side produces a different sound when struck with a mallet.

Jingle Sticks   Jingle sticks are easily made by hammering flattened-out bottle caps onto a thin strip of quarter-inch wood (see Figure 4.13). When shaken, they sound like tambourines or commercial jingle sticks.

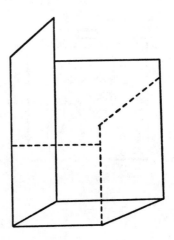

Figure 4.12   Hollow Box

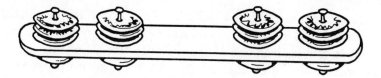

Figure 4.13   Self-Made Jingle Stick

The log drum (Figure 4.14) is an African instrument made by gluing wood together to form a rectangular, hollow box. Before the top is glued on, three slits are drilled or cut out of it to form a lopsided, sideways H. When the two tongues (labeled A and B on the drawing) are struck with a mallet, each produces a separate, distinct pitch. The sound of the longer tongue is lower than that of the shorter tongue.   *Log Drum*

Clay flowerpots also make lovely instruments. A wide variety of sizes is desirable since flowerpots of different sizes make different sounds. A cord is threaded through the hole on the bottom of each pot and knotted on the inside to form a handle. The performer holds the pot by the cord and strikes it with a mallet, producing a ringing tone. The pots can also be suspended from a wooden frame.   *Flowerpots*

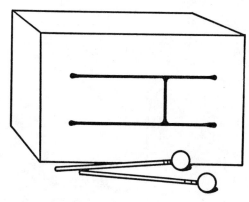

Figure 4.14   Log Drum

Lion's Roar or Dog Bark   A lion's roar is made by poking a small hole in the head of a drum. Next, rosin is rubbed onto a skewer, wooden dowel, or string, which is then inserted into the hole. Pulling the skewer or string in and out creates a sound reminiscent of a roar or bark. (Children experiment with this sort of device in fast food restaurants when they pull their straws in and out of the lids on their drink cups.) Imagine the excitement children would experience using this instrument to accompany songs about animals.

Middle Eastern Drum   A middle eastern drum (Figure 4.15) can be made by potters or people experienced with working with clay. A funnel-shaped drum frame is formed and fired. The bottom of the funnel must be wide enough for a hand to be inserted. A skin head is mounted onto the frame with a metal rim. The drum is played with two hands. One hand hits the drumhead, and the other moves in and out of the open end to vary the pitch. A beautiful, exotic sound is produced.

Pottery Disks   A lovely sounding instrument can be created by suspending assorted sizes of pottery disk (see Figure 4.16). The disks must have a hole in them so that they can be suspended and vibrate freely. The disks can be suspended individually, or several can be attached to the same cord.

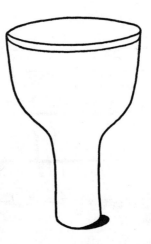

Figure 4.15   Middle-Eastern Drum

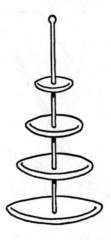

Figure 4.16 Pottery Disks

The whip-crack is made with three pieces of quarter-inch *Whip-Crack* wood and a hinge. The length of the wood can vary, but an instrument about twelve inches long and two inches wide is probably a good size for children. Two strips of wood are cut to the same length. The top board is sawed into two pieces so that one piece is about three inches long and the other piece nine inches long. The two cut pieces are then hinged together to form the top. The shorter length of wood is glued to the bottom strip of wood to form a handle (See Figure 4.17). The whip-crack is played by flicking the wrist so that the hinged top piece of wood slaps against the bottom piece, creating a sharp crack. This instrument is used in the orchestra to create the sound of a whip crack in pieces such as Leroy Anderson's "Sleigh Ride." Children may decide to use the whip-crack to create sound effects in songs about such things as storms, rockets, or woodworking.

The slapstick (Figure 4.18) is virtually the same instrument *Slapstick* as the whip-crack, and it creates the same sound. Two strips of wood are hinged together at the bottom. Handles are mounted on the outer side of each piece of wood several inches away from the hinge. The pieces of wood are slapped together by the performer holding the handles.

All these instruments are relatively simple and inexpensive **Conclusion** to make. Teachers may find parents willing to take the time

81

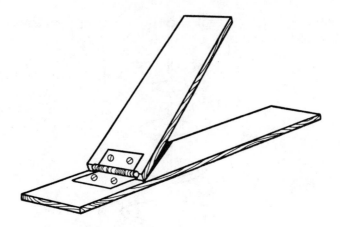

Figure 4.17   Self-Made Whip Crack

to construct some of them. Some schools have had work parties where parents bring a potluck dinner and socialize while they work. Having so many unique but beautiful sounding percussion instruments encourages children to experiment with sound and think creatively about the relationship between sound and music.

PURCHASING AND STORING INSTRUMENTS

Instruments can be purchased either at music stores or through catalogs. Music stores have the advantage that the instruments can be tried out before they are selected, but

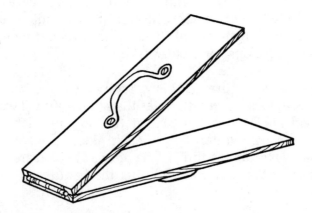

Figure 4.18   Self-Made Slapstick

catalogs may offer a greater selection. Some music stores and catalog companies give a discount to schools.

The best-quality melody and percussion (rhythm) instruments are often identified by manufacturers as being for use with the Orff method. High-quality melody instruments can also be identified by their wooden frames, assortment of sizes, and movable bars. Their good sound and durability make them worth the higher cost.

Storage of instruments is an important consideration if they are to last and maintain their tone quality. The biggest enemies of musical instruments are heat and moisture. Excessive heat causes wood to warp and crack, drumheads to dry out and crack, and strings to break. Moisture causes wood to warp and metal to rust. Therefore, instruments should be stored in a dry place away from heat. (Excessive dryness can also damage instruments. If the air is very dry, jars of water can be placed in the storage area, as long as they will not fall over onto the instruments!)

Instruments also should be stored so that other instruments are not piled on top of them. It is safest to store instruments of the same type together—tone blocks in one container, bells in another, triangles in another. Then there is no need to worry about the bells scratching the tone blocks or the triangles getting caught in the bells. This also helps children learn to categorize the instruments as they help put the instruments away. The worst way to store instruments is in a communal box, where they quickly become broken or damaged.

Children need to learn appropriate ways to handle instruments just as they do other materials. When collecting instruments after a group music period, the teacher can pass around the instrument container so that each child can carefully place his or her instrument in the container, rather than throwing it into a box. If several types of instruments have been used, the teacher might have the children come up a few at a time to place their instruments in the appropriate container.

Teachers can encourage children to explore sound and create music by having instruments available as an integral part of the classroom. In this way children can experiment with the **INSTRUMENTS THROUGHOUT THE DAY** sounds various instruments produce. In addition, songs can be sung spontaneously while children accompany on instruments. It is important for the teacher to verbalize or help children talk about how the different materials sound. Also, teachers and children can discuss how the way an instrument is played affects the sound. For example: "You hit the tambourine very hard and it sounded loud. Then you tapped it softly, and I could barely hear it."

Or: "Did you notice that when Billy played the xylophone with the felt mallet, it sounded different from when he used the wood mallet? Billy, will you do that again so we can listen more carefully?"

Such concepts, which seem obvious to adults, are not necessarily apparent to children. The teacher cannot assume that a three- or four-year-old necessarily understands the relationship between how hard you strike an instrument and how loud it sounds. As an example of how children fail to see this relationship, a group of three-year-olds was experimenting with an autoharp. The teacher remarked that one child was playing the autoharp softly and asked what she would need to do to make it loud. The child confidently replied, "Push another button!"

The teacher should decide which instruments to place in the child's environment just as he or she plans which materials to make available in all areas of the curriculum. Some questions a teacher might ask in deciding which instruments to display are:

- Will a wooden instrument and a metal instrument be placed in the room so that the children can compare the sounds of the two?
- Will a large drum and a small drum be introduced so that the children can see how size affects sound?
- Has the teacher heard some of the children making up songs? Putting a melody instrument out might encourage this.

When these questions have been answered, the teacher can select which instrument or instruments to incorporate into the classroom environment. As the children experiment with the instruments, they will be developing science concepts, language, and fine-motor skills, as well as an understanding and appreciation of music.

SUMMARY

A great variety of instruments are available to the teacher of young children. In addition to the large assortment of rhythm instruments, there are melody instruments and accompanying instruments.

Instruments are an important part of music groups with both nursery school and primary school children. They can be used to augment songs, perform rhythmic patterns, stimulate movement, and create songs. In addition to their use in group situations, instruments should be an integral part of the classroom environment so that the children have an opportunity to experiment with them throughout the day. This will facilitate the development of concepts about the nature of sound and music.

NOTES

1. Note that all the songs in this book have autoharp chords indicated in the music.

2. Professor Otte's instrument is tuned so that each half-step (see Glossary) is divided into three equal parts. For classroom use it is not necessary to construct the instrument with exactly this tuning system.

3. Such a precise measurement is necessary because at these points the pipe does not vibrate; such a place is called a *node*. If the holes are not placed at the nodes, the vibration of the pipe will be dampened and the resonance adversely affected.

4. A marimba resembles a xylophone, but its bars are wider and flatter, creating a mellower tone. In addition, marimbas have metal tubes beneath the wooden bars to increase resonance. Although this self-made instrument does not have such resonating tubes, its tone resembles that of a marimba.

SELECTED BIBLIOGRAPHY

Bartlett, Harry R. *Guide to Teaching Percussion*, 2nd ed. by Ronald A. Holloway. Dubuque, Iowa: Wm. C. Brown, 1971.

Fletcher, Helen Jill. *The First Book of Bells.* New York: Franklin Watts, 1959.

Garnett, Hugh. *Musical Instruments You Can Make.* London: Pittman Publishing, 1976.

Marsh, Mary Val; Rinehart, Carroll; Savage, Edith; Beelke, Ralph; and Silverman, Ronald. *The Spectrum of Music*, Vol. I. New York: Macmillan, 1974.

Surplus, Robert W. *The Beat of the Drum.* Minneapolis: Lerner Publications, 1963.

🌿 5
Movement

MOVEMENT IS intrinsic to the developing child. Toddlers seem to be in constant motion, and even older children alternate quiet periods with times of feverish activity. Teachers of young children should give careful attention to this need for movement. Planned movement activities can help children develop in many ways.

First of all, movement experiences help children in their overall gross-motor development. Since movement activities give children an opportunity to explore their bodies in relation to space, they are valuable in developing body awareness. In addition, creative movement provides an outlet for emotional release in both children and adults, and encourages children to think imaginatively. Finally, movement within the context of a music experience helps children acquire a feel for the rhythm and mood of the music.

Young children can be involved with creative movement in a variety of ways. They can create movements to go with music, perform various dramatic movements not necessarily accompanied by music, create specific movements associated with certain rhythms, dramatize stories, or perform dances.

Several types of music encourage children to create dramatic movement. First, many songs deal with topics that can be

MOVEMENT TO MUSIC

acted out. Certain classical pieces[1] also encourage creative movement. In addition, some children's records specifically stimulate dramatic movement.

Songs   Many songs lend themselves well to dramatization by children. The content of some songs invites movement so strongly that children may get up spontaneously and begin to act out the song. Children enjoy moving to songs that dramatize characters, suggest action, or create a specific mood.

Dramatizing Characters   Many songs written for young children deal with people or animals familiar to the children. Songs about mail carriers, construction workers, dogs, cats, zoo animals, and so on are easy for children to reenact because they deal with familiar subject matter. The song "Old MacDonald Had a Farm" mentions many animals that children can imitate. "Fire Truck Song" (Example 5.1) and "The Turtle" (Example 5.2) are two songs that could be used for dramatization.

In "Fire Truck Song" the children can act out the fire fighters driving the truck and putting out the fire. The children can also add new words to the song, such as:

> Firemen put the ladders up . . .
> Firemen get the hoses out . . .
> Firemen spray the water on . . .
> Firemen climb the ladders . . .

These added words stimulate additional actions to use in portraying fire fighters.

In "The Turtle," the teacher may want to ask the children what things the turtle can do besides crawling. Children might decide to imitate turtles sleeping, swimming, snapping at flies, and so on.

Another good song for reenactment is "The Hippopotamus" (Example 2.20). If the children have been to the zoo and seen a hippopotamus or have read about one in a book, they may have other ideas to add to this song. They may want to reenact the way the hippopotamus swam or tried to catch peanuts.

Dramatizing Action   Other songs emphasize action rather than characters. Consequently, the children imitate the specific action suggested

Example 5.1
FIRE TRUCK SONG

Original key: E-flat

Daniel Hooley

Ding ding ding ding ding! Here comes the fire truck, the fire truck!

Ding ding ding ding ding! Get out of the way!

Fire-men put the fire out! Fire-men put the fire out!

Ding ding ding ding ding! There goes the fire truck, the fire truck!

Ding ding ding ding ding! Get out of the way!

Source: From *Sharing Music*, Level K of the MUSIC FOR YOUNG
AMERICANS series by Richard Berg et al., Copyright ©1966 (Cincinnati:
American Book Company). Reprinted by permission of American Book
Company.

Example 5.2
THE TURTLE

Ethel Crowninshield

The tur-tle tra-vels slow-ly, His house is on his back.

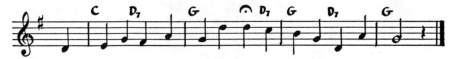

And you would tra-vel slow-ly too, If you had such a pack.

Source: Ethel Crowninshield, *New Songs and Games* (Boston: Boston
Music Company, 1941). Used by permission of the copyright owner: THE
BOSTON MUSIC COMPANY, Boston, MA 02216.

in the song. "Autumn Leaves" (Example 2.7) is one such song. The children can reenact the leaves falling, turning, blowing, and being raked.

"What Shall We Do" (Example 5.3) incorporates a variety of characters or objects with their corresponding movements. Children can add their own ideas to this song about toys and then act them out.

TAPE
(1st & 3rd verses)

Example 5.3
WHAT SHALL WE DO

Original key: D   Mary Jaye

2. We'll play with toys on a winter's day . . .
   . . . , When we can't go out and play.

3. I'm a steam shovel and I dig, dig, dig . . .
   . . . , I dig on a winter's day.

4. I'm a rocket ship and I zoom, zoom, zoom . . .
   . . . , I zoom on a winter's day.

5. I'm a spinning wheel and I whirl . . .

6. I'm a ballerina and I dance . . .

7. I'm a big robot and I walk . . .

A third type of song evokes a particular mood that may encourage children to express themselves through movement. Such songs often deal with nature, the seasons, or feelings. "The North Wind's Song" (Example 5.4) has a subdued, slightly melancholy feeling that children may want to translate into movement.

Dramatizing Mood

In contrast, "It's So Good" (Example 5.5) may make the children feel happy and boisterous. After they have sung the song, the teacher may want to ask them to move the way the song makes them feel.

Much classical music also inspires dramatization. For example, some well-known orchestral music was written to represent particular animals or aspects of nature. Presenting this music in conjunction with the story or object it represents, and inviting the children to dramatize the music, is an excellent way to introduce children to orchestral music. It also emphasizes creativity of movement. The following three examples deal with subject matter that can be reenacted by the children in their own way.

Classical Music

- Saint-Saëns, *Carnival of the Animals*. This familiar orchestral piece includes many animals familiar to young children.
- Mussorgsky/Ravel, "Ballet of the Chicks in Their Shells" from *Pictures at an Exhibition*.
- Debussy, "Nuages" ("Clouds") from *Nocturnes*.

TAPE

Example 5.4
THE NORTH WIND'S SONG

Original key: E minor   Josephine Wolverton

Ooo   Ooo,   the   North Wind sings a   lone-some tune.

Ooo,   Ooo,   cold   win-ter's com- ing   soon.

Source: From *Sharing Music*, Level K of the MUSIC FOR YOUNG AMERICANS series by Richard Berg et al., Copyright ©1966 (Cincinnati: American Book Company). Reprinted by permission of American Book Company.

Example 5.5
IT'S SO GOOD

Sally Moomaw

It's so good to see ev-ery-one to-day. It's so

good to see ev-ery-one to-day.

Ja-son and Ann and Da-vid and Steph-an-ie, It's so

good to see ev-ery-one to-day!

Copyright ©1979, 1980 by Sally Coup Moomaw.

Classical music need not tell a story or represent a particular object in order to be dramatized. Many pieces evoke a mood that children can translate into creative movement. For example, the opening to Tchaikovsky's *Fourth Symphony* is martial in character and may inspire marching. The children may alter their movements as the music changes but return to marching whenever the original theme returns.

Sometimes props encourage children to move their bodies to the sound of the music. Scarves, ribbons, and streamers are often used. One class waved streamers as they swayed and danced to "Morning" from Grieg's *Peer Gynt Suite #1*. Another class used spiral spring toys to accompany music.[2] Feathers and hoops also make good props.

Children's Action Records

A number of fine children's records encourage movement. Some of these records emphasize creative or dramatic movement by suggesting a topic for dramatization, such as various animals walking.[3] Others have songs with specific directions for the children to follow and thus encourage the development of listening skills and vocabulary. Both types of records are good to use with young children since they focus on different aspects of development.

Age Levels and Movement to Music

Infants and Toddlers

Infants who are wide awake often respond to singing by moving their bodies. (When they are drowsy, singing may have the opposite effect and put them to sleep!) This is even more noticeable in toddlers, who may respond to music by bouncing, clapping, and tottering around. Dramatizing specific characters, creating specific movements, and acting out moods are too abstract for most toddlers.

Preschool Children

Three-, four-, and five-year-olds enjoy creating movements to dramatize characters and actions in songs and other music. Children of this age are often less inhibited than they will be later in the primary grades, so this is a golden age for giving children the freedom to recreate what they observe in their environment. Dramatizing moods is more abstract than reenacting characters or actions and thus may be difficult for many preschool children.

Preschool children also enjoy following the directions on action records. Whereas dramatizing characters, actions, or feelings focuses on creativity of movement and imagination, following the directions on movement records helps children develop listening skills and vocabulary as well as large-muscle skills. Both activities are valuable.

Primary-Age Children

Most children in kindergarten and first grade still enjoy dramatizing music. As with preschool children, the teacher should respect the feelings of those who do not enjoy it and not try to force them into activities that do not interest them or make them feel uncomfortable. As they grow older, some children begin to feel embarrassed by these activities, and the teacher should be sensitive to this.

There are movement activities that appeal to older primary children as well as to younger children. Many children in the primary grades delight in creating dramatizations to movement records. Some of these records deal with topics, such as pizza dough, that are fun for this age group.[4] Primary children are often more capable of recreating moods in songs

93

than are preschoolers. In addition, because primary children are interested in following rules, they may be interested in more structured movements. The class could decide how they want to choreograph a piece of music if most children do not seem to be performing spontaneous movement.

DRAMATIC MOVEMENT

Children can perform many types of dramatic movement that are not necessarily included in songs. In fact, children may have more freedom to express themselves through movement when they do not have to fit their actions into the confines of a song.

The list of things that children can dramatize is limited only by the bounds of their experiences or imaginations. When considering ideas for dramatization, the teacher should consider what experiences the children have had recently that have interested them. The teacher can also ask the children what they would like to act out.

The following is an abbreviated list of things that children can dramatize. It is meant to be a catalyst to help teachers develop ideas that are relevant to their own groups of children.

- Pretend you are a balloon being blown up.
- Imitate plants growing.
- Dramatize freezing and thawing.
- Fall like a beanbag, then fall like a feather.
- Dramatize popcorn sizzling in a pan and then popping.
- Blast off like a rocket.
- Walk like robots.
- Slither like worms.
- Act out a fishing sequence.
- Dramatize getting dressed for a walk in the snow.
- Join children together with each child holding the waist of the child ahead of him to create a pretend centipede.
- Recreate a field trip to the zoo.
- Pretend you are a wheel.

Some of these activities are single activities, such as falling like a beanbag. Others require the children to relate experiences in sequence, such as getting dressed for a walk in the snow. Both encourage creativity in movement, but the latter also helps develop memory and time sequencing.

Certain rhythms are traditionally accompanied by particular movements. Learning to associate these rhythms and their corresponding movements helps children develop their ability to perceive rhythms and their feel for music. Music with these specific patterns has been recorded on numerous records that clearly indicate which type of movement goes with which music. Teachers can also play these rhythms on rhythm instruments or on the autoharp. Example 5.6 shows some typical rhythmic patterns and the movements associated with them. (Words have been added to assist teachers who do not read music in performing the rhythm. The words are not meant to be used with the children, however, since this would discourage them from hearing the actual music.)

Movements to Specific Rhythms

Example 5.6
Rhythmic patterns associated with various movements

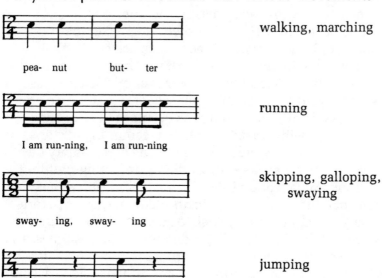

walking, marching

pea- nut   but- ter

running

I am run-ning,   I am run-ning

skipping, galloping, swaying

sway- ing,   sway- ing

jumping

jump (silence)   jump (silence)

Age Levels and Movement to Specific Rhythms

The types of movements children can perform depend on their level of large-motor development. Most two-year-olds can walk, run, and sway to music. Three-year-olds can do all these and also march, jump, and gallop to music. Some four-year-olds and most five-year-olds can skip to music. Most primary-age children can perform all these movements but the teacher may need to help a few with skipping.

DRAMATIZING STORIES

Another way of encouraging young children to move creatively is to have them dramatize stories. Some music books provide stories with music to accompany them. The teacher reads the narration, and the teacher and children sing the songs as interested children dramatize the story.

Teachers can also select some of the children's favorite books that lend themselves well to dramatization and encourage the children to make up songs to accompany the story. *The Carrot Seed* is a good story to dramatize.[5] Children can portray all the characters in the story and even reenact the carrot growing. This book also has a record to accompany it, which contains the narration plus some amusing songs.

Lost Bear, Found Bear is another good book to dramatize.[6] The children can act out the various characters and can also compose songs for each character to sing.

Teachers can write their own stories for children to dramatize. In this way the teacher can select a topic that is relevant to the interest of the children. The children can also write stories for dramatization. For example, if the class has been on a field trip recently, the teacher might have a group of interested children recount the events of the trip and then reenact it, possibly to music. Such a recounting of stories or important events encourages sequencing and memory development, as well as creative thinking, in young children.

Story dramatization is too abstract for most toddlers, but three- or four-year-olds begin to enjoy acting out stories. Primary-age children may wish to go beyond simple dramatizations and make a small production with costumes and props. They also may enjoy creating their own operettas by writing stories and selecting or composing music to accompany them.

Dancing is popular with people from toddlerhood to adulthood. Some particular dances are appropriate for each age level.

Toddlers enjoy free movement or making up their own dances to music. Two-year-olds may also enjoy some very simple dances such as "Step and Clap" (Example 5.7) if they are performed slowly enough for them to keep up.

Toddlers

Children ages three to five also enjoy dances. They can make up their own dances to music or perform dances such as the "Hokey Pokey" (Example 2.16). A dance of an entirely different type is "A Gust of Fall Wind" (Example 5.8). It has simple but lovely movements that preschool children can perform.

Preschool Children

Children in the primary grades are at a stage of development where they enjoy rule games, so dances with specific steps or movements appeal to them. The two examples listed work well with first-graders. Second- and third-graders can begin to do dances with more complicated steps. The polka is a

Primary-Age Children

TAPE

Example 5.7
STEP AND CLAP

Original key: G

Elsie Smith, music
Anne Beyer, lyrics

Step step clap clap, step step clap clap,

Turn your-self a-round and then you clap clap clap.

Source: From *Sharing Music*, Level K of the MUSIC FOR YOUNG AMERICANS series by Richard Berg et al., Copyright ©1966 (Cincinnati: American Book Company). Reprinted by permission of American Book Company.

Example 5.8
A GUST OF FALL WIND

Original key: D   Chinese-American folk song

A gust of fall wind blow- ing cold.
(Raise arms. Swing them gracefully from right to left to indicate blowing wind.)

A fall of white dew turned to frost.
(With arms still raised, go down on both knees to touch the frozen ground.)

The cruel frost free-zes each blade of grass,
(Cross hands over the chest to indicate the cold.)

And the grass- hop-per dies in his gras- sy nest.
(Spread arms upward and outward and sink to the ground as the grasshopper dies.)

Source: Words and music from A. Gertrude Jacobs, compiler, *Chinese-American Song and Game Book* (San Diego: A.S. Barnes, 1944). Reprinted by permission of copyright owner, Consolidated Publishing Corporation. Movement directions from *Making Music Your Own 2* (Morristown, N.J.: Silver Burdett Company, 1968), Copyright ©1971 General Learning Corporation. Reprinted by permission of Silver Burdett Company.

good dance to introduce at this stage. Children can practice by galloping to the music, leading first with the right foot and then with the left. Next they can do one three-step gallop with the right foot, then one three-step gallop with the left foot. To perform the polka, two children join hands and begin alternating polka steps. The partner on the right starts the polka with the right foot leading, and the one on the left starts the polka with the left foot leading. Together they polka around the room with each person alternating the lead foot. "Do You Know the Muffin Man?" (Example 5.9) is a good song to accompany a polka. The words can be altered to include the names and addresses of the children in the class. For example:

Example 5.9
DO YOU KNOW THE MUFFIN MAN

Traditional

Do you know the muf-fin man, the muf-fin man, the muf-fin man?

Do you know the muf-fin man, who lives in Dru-ry Lane?

Do you know Susan, Susan, Susan,
Do you know Susan, she lives on Market Street?

For another version of this song, see Example 10.1.

Some of the dances and game songs commonly used with preschool and primary children require the children to select other children for participation in the song. An example is the familiar "Farmer in the Dell." Inevitably some children will be the last to be selected, which can lead to a lowering of their self-esteem. Since there are many other enjoyable dances and game songs that do not foster competition among the children, it seems wise to select these in preference to those that involve children selecting other children. It is also best to select dances and games that involve all the children rather than those that involve only a select few with the rest mainly watching.

As with the other areas of music, creative movement should be coordinated with the rest of the curriculum. If the children are studying fall, creative movements to imitate falling leaves and nuts, raking leaves, or birds flying would be appropriate. If the class has been on a field trip recently, dramatizing some of the things the children saw on the trip provides a good follow-up activity.

MOVEMENT THROUGHOUT THE DAY

Dramatic movement should not be confined to a music class or movement group. The teacher should take cues from the children throughout the day and select movements that correspond to their immediate interests. If children are watching fish swim in a bowl, the teacher might ask if they can imitate the movements of the fish. If the children notice a grasshopper jumping outside, that is an appropriate time to initiate jumping activities.

Movement activities are very stimulating to young children and may quickly get out of control in the close confines of the classroom. If the teacher sees this happening, the children can be redirected to performing these movements outside or in a large-motor-development room if one is available. If the teacher does not have access to an outside area or a large-muscle room for immediate redirection of the children, then perhaps the children could act out the movement with their hands and later, when there is room, use their whole bodies. In this way the teacher does not lose the opportunity to help the children experience the movements of the object of interest to them at the moment.

Using the fishbowl example, the teacher might note that the room is crowded and there is no room for the children to act out the movements of the fish. Therefore, the teacher might say: "Look how the fish are swimming and how their mouths move. Do you think you can move your mouth like the fish? Let's see if we can make our hands move the way the fish's body moves." Later, when the children are outside, the teacher might suggest: "Do you remember how the fish looked when we watched them swimming in the bowl? Do you think you can make your bodies move like the fish?"

MANAGING MOVEMENT GROUPS

Some teachers, in addition to encouraging movement throughout the day, like to have a special movement group experience each day for interested children. Other teachers have a group music experience for interested children and incorporate movement into that activity. Before starting either of these activities, the teacher must make certain that there is adequate room for the children to move.

Group movement activities sometimes create management problems in the classroom that can be avoided if the teacher anticipates the situation and decides how to handle it in advance. Some types of movement are by their nature louder and more boisterous activities than others. For example, children acting out bears are apt to be much louder and more active than children pretending to be turtles. If the teacher is planning a stimulating activity such as acting out bears, part of the planning should include helping the children calm down so they can move to the next activity. The teacher might end the bear movement by suggesting that the bears go to sleep or by planning a quiet movement activity to follow the more active movement period. The teacher could tell the children that first they will pretend to be bears, and then snails. The teacher and children could discuss ahead of time how bears move and sound and how snails move and sound. Once the children have been calmed down by the quieter activity, the teacher can more easily gain their attention and help them make the transition to a new activity.

Some children join in movement activities readily; others prefer to watch. Many of these watchers gradually become more comfortable in the group and begin to participate, but others never do. The teacher should respect the feelings of those who do not want to participate and should not try to force them. Forcing a reluctant child into a movement activity can cause the child anxiety and lower his or her self-esteem.

Movement activities are an important part of the preschool **SUMMARY** and primary curriculum. They help children develop gross motor skills and body awareness, provide an emotional release, and assist children in developing a feel for rhythm and mood in music. Teachers can plan activities that encourage children to dramatize music, create dramatic movements to imitate familiar things in their environment, perform specific movements to rhythms, act out stories, and dance. Although the teacher may wish to plan group movement activities or encompass movement in a regular music group, movement should also be encouraged throughout the day and incorporated into the daily curriculum.

1. Although the Classical period of music history refers **NOTES** specifically to music of the second half of the eighteenth century— the period of Franz Josef Haydn (1732–1809) and Wolfgang

Amadeus Mozart (1756–1791)—the term *classical* is used in common parlance to refer to all music written in this tradition. For lack of a better term, *classical* is used here in this all-encompassing sense.

2. Appreciation is expressed to Dawn Denno for her ideas on using spring toys.

3. Maya Doray, "Make Believe in Movement," (Long Beach, N.J.: Kimbo Educational Recording, 1976). KIM0500.

4. Georgiana Liccione Stewart, "Walk Like the Animals" (Long Beach, N.J.: Kimbo Educational Recording, 1976). KIM7040.

5. Ruth Krauss, *The Carrot Seed* (New York: Harper and Row, 1945).

6. Patrick Mayers, *Lost Bear, Found Bear* (Chicago: Albert Whitman and Company, 1973).

SELECTED BIBLIOGRAPHY

Bley, Edgar S. *The Best Singing Games for Children of All Ages.* New York: Sterling Publishing Company, 1978.

Cherry, Clare. *Creative Movement for the Developing Child,* rev. ed. Belmont, Calif.: Fearon Publishers, 1971.

Doray, Maya. *Make Believe in Movement.* Long Beach, N.J.: Kimbo Educational Recording, 1976. KIM0500

Dubsky, Dora. *Sing and Dance.* New York: Stephen Daye Press, 1955.

Findlay, Elsa. *Rhythm and Movement, Applications of Dalcroze Eurhythmics.* Evanston, Ill.: Summy-Birchard Company, 1971.

Gray, Vera, and Percival, Rachel. *Music, Movement, and Mime for Children.* London: Oxford University Press, 1962.

Hofman, Charles, *American Indians Sing.* New York: John Day Company, 1967.

Stewart, Georgiana Liccione. *Walk Like the Animals.* Long Beach, N.J.: Kimbo Educational Recording, 1976. KIM7040

Wilson, Harry R.; Ehret, Walter; Knuth, Alice M.; Hermann, Edward J.; and Renna, Albert A. *Growing with Music,* Vols. 1 and 2. Englewood Cliffs, N.J.: Prentice-Hall, 1970.

Wuytack, Joseph, and Arron, Tosi. *Play, Sing, and Dance.* Paris: Alphonse Leduc, 1972.

6
Listening

CHILDREN BENEFIT from listening activities in several ways. First, listening activities help children focus on sound and develop auditory discrimination, which is crucial to their later ability to sound out and read words. Second, exposure to a variety of music increases children's enjoyment of music and understanding of sound. Finally, experimenting with sound helps children formulate concepts of sound and music.

A wide variety of listening experiences can be incorporated into the classroom. Guests can be brought in to sing or play instruments. Children can listen to various types of records or to teacher-made recordings of themselves or of familiar sounds in the classroom; they can play listening games and experiment with sound; and they can paint or write to music. Finally, teachers can encourage children to listen to sounds throughout the day.

GUESTS
Procedures for Guests

The best way to interest children in listening to music is to have a guest visit the class to sing or perform on an instrument. It is much easier for children to listen to a live performance than to a recorded one, and seeing an instrument played helps them associate a particular sound with the instrument that produces it. Once children have heard a live performance on an instrument, they are more interested in hearing that instrument on a recording and have a better understanding of what they are hearing.

Parents are sometimes good guests for musical performances. Some parents may have played an instrument in their high school band or orchestra, and they may be delighted to play it for the children. Other parents may enjoy singing with the children.

Another source of talent for live presentations is the local high school. Talented students may be willing to sing or demonstrate their instruments; if the school approves, this could be a rewarding experience for both the young children and the performer. If there is a local college, teachers might want to ask whether any students are willing to perform for the children. Some college music instructors encourage their students to perform in public as often as possible and would recommend students to demonstrate their instruments.

Guests will probably need some coaching from the teacher on how to present their instruments. The teacher might suggest that they show how high and low the instrument can play, demonstrate the various things that the instrument can do, and talk about how the sound is produced. Then the guest performer might play a short piece on the instrument. Enough time should be allowed for the children to ask questions about the instrument. The teacher should ask the performer ahead of time whether the children will be allowed to touch the instrument, hold it, or try to play it. Before the performer arrives, the teacher can convey to the children what types of things they will be able to do with the instrument.

Age Levels and Guests
Infants and Toddlers

Infants and toddlers are, of course, too young to observe concert etiquette, but they are immensely interested in sound and are usually thrilled to hear someone play an instrument. Many towns and cities sponsor outdoor band or orchestra concerts to which parents can take their children without worrying about the sounds the children may make. When the infants or toddlers get tired or lose interest, the parents can leave easily without disturbing other people.

If infants and toddlers are being cared for in a child care center, guests can be brought in for more informal presentations than would normally be planned for older children. The guests can come into the room, quietly sit down, and begin playing. Interested children can come over to listen and observe and can leave as they lose interest. Naturally, this process would have to be worked out in advance with the guest. If the instrument is a loud one, the children will need to be warned before the performer begins playing so that they will not be frightened.

Preschool Children

Three-, four-, and five-year-olds are usually ready to sit quietly for short performances. Since the attention spans of individual children vary, the teacher should decide in advance how children who grow restless will be handled. Perhaps another quiet activity in the room could be provided, or the child might be able to play in another room until the demonstration is over. Sometimes just having an adult sit next to a restless child and perhaps rub his or her back enables the child to calm down enough to enjoy the performance.

Primary-Age Children

Children in the primary grades usually have longer attention spans than preschoolers do and are more accustomed to sitting quietly for periods of time. Therefore, they may enjoy a slightly longer demonstration or even a short concert. They are also better able to sit quietly even if they would prefer to leave. The teacher might talk with the children about how the performer feels when an audience is loud or restless, since children of this age can begin to take another person's point of view.

LISTENING AREAS IN THE CLASSROOM

Teachers can encourage children to listen to music by providing an atmosphere and environment that are conducive to listening. Ideally, a separate area of the classroom should be designed for that purpose. Such an area should be relatively quiet and comfortable, and have a minimum number of distractions. The area might be partly blocked off from the rest of the room to cut down on noise and confusion and to increase privacy. Such an area might also contain large cushions and a rocking chair for comfort. A record player and/or cassette recorder could be available with interesting things to listen to, and earphones might be provided for primary-age children. A lamp would add coziness to the area.

Such a restful, cozy spot within a classroom encourages children to stay for a while, relax, and listen.

LISTENING TO RECORDS

Listening to a recording of an instrument that has previously been demonstrated in class is an excellent follow-up activity for children. Because they have already seen and heard the instrument, they can relate the listening activity to the concrete experience of hearing the instrument in person, and thus can better understand what they are hearing. If the teacher takes a photograph of the performer who visited the class along with the instrument and displays the photograph in the classroom, the children will have a visual reminder of the experience to associate with the aural reminder of the recording.

Various types of records can be used successfully with young children: story records, vocal records, classical records, folk records, jazz records, and the children's own records.

Story Records

The perennial favorite among story records for children is Prokofiev's *Peter and the Wolf*. Besides holding the children's attention through the story line, it is also a good introduction to the instruments of the orchestra and a highly rated piece of music by a well-known composer. Older children might enjoy acting out this piece after listening.

There are many other story records for use with young children. The teacher should preview each record before introducing it into the classroom in order to be sure the content fits with the teacher's philosophy. For example, "Tubby the Tuba," a popular story record for children, is a clever story with interesting music, nicely performed.[1] It does, however, convey the idea that the instruments of the orchestra play themselves. This might be misleading to children still attempting to sort out the difference between reality and fantasy.

Vocal Records

A large variety of vocal records are available for use with young children. The teacher might consider selecting records that relate to other areas of the curriculum. There are recordings dealing with transportation, children's feelings, nature, space, classroom games, animals, children of other lands, community workers, and so forth. The teacher should listen to any record chosen before using it in the classroom to make certain the content of the song is appropriate and the performance acceptable.

Classical Records

Adults often feel that young children will relate only to children's records or story records, but this does not appear to be the case. Children who are introduced to classical music at an early age often enjoy this music as much as or even more than other music. One two-year-old who had been exposed to both classical music and story records selected Stravinsky's *Pulcinella* as his favorite and insisted on hearing it every day. Another two-year-old especially enjoyed "conducting" Tchaikovsky's *Fifth Symphony*, but at age three abruptly switched to Respighi's *Pines of Rome* and played it incessantly. Yet another two-year-old demanded "the harpsichord record" every day, and a twenty-month-old asked for anything with a "biolin."

The aforementioned musical works are not on the list of records traditionally presented as good ones for introducing young children to classical music; yet they were selected by the children themselves as their favorites. For this reason it is difficult to suggest which specific records may be the best ones to use with young children. In general, children seem to be more readily attracted to louder, quicker music than to quieter, slower music. Music with percussive effects such as cymbal crashes also especially interests them. In addition, music that features instruments with interesting tone qualities, such as the harpsichord, seems to attract young listeners. Because children's tastes are so variable, it is best if the teacher introduces a wide variety of orchestral and instrumental pieces and lets the children select those they particularly like. For teachers who want more guidance than these broad suggestions, a list of classical works that often appeal to young children follows. Again, however, it must be emphasized that many children will prefer music not included on this list. The more recordings the teacher can acquire for the classroom, the more likely the children are to find music that appeals to them individually. The public library is an excellent source of classical recordings.

The following is a short list of possible classical pieces to use with young children.

- Bach, J. S. — *Brandenburg Concerto #2*
- Britten — *A Young Person's Guide to the Orchestra*

- Copland—*Billy the Kid*
- Dvořák—*Carnival Overture*
- Grieg—*Peer Gynt Suite #1*
- Mozart—*Eine Kleine Nachtmusik* ("A Little Night Music")
- Mussorgsky/Ravel—*Pictures at an Exhibition*
- Rameau—*Les Indes Galantes*
- Ravel—*Ma Mère l'Oye* ("Mother Goose")
- Rossini—*William Tell Overture*
- Saint-Saëns—*Carnival of the Animals*
- Scarlatti, D.—*Harpsichord Sonatas*
- Stravinsky—*Firebird*
- Tchaikovsky—*Fourth* and *Fifth Symphonies*

Folk Records   Folk records are appealing to many young children. The simple melodies and repeated verses seem to attract them. As with other vocal music, the teacher should listen to the songs before using them in the classroom to make sure their content is not frightening or confusing to young children. For example, the song "I Know an Old Lady Who Swallowed a Fly" suggests that the old lady may die from swallowing the fly.[2] This is frightening to some young children, who fear that they may die from swallowing an insect.

Jazz Records   Many jazz records are also appealing to young children and will expand their musical horizons. Jazz records may be overstimulating to some children, so the teacher may need to assess the activity level in the classroom carefully before playing jazz recordings. The teacher may need to set some limits on the type of movement that will be permitted, or limit the size of the group if free movement will be allowed.

Children's Own Records   Children often want to bring their own records to school to play for the other children. This is an excellent way to interest children in listening to music and a good way of sharing the music of different cultures. In addition, it builds self-esteem in the child who brings the record. The teacher, of course, has to decide whether the record is suitable for other children to hear. A child bringing a record to school is offering to share an important part of him- or herself, so considerable latitude should be observed in allowing children's records into the classroom. If a record is clearly unacceptable, the teacher must use extreme tact in explaining to the child why the record cannot be played for the class. For example, if a child brings a very scary monster record to school, the teacher might say: "It was so thoughtful of you to bring your own record for us to hear. This must be a record you really enjoy, and you want us to enjoy it too. Thank you for showing it to me. I can't play your record in class because I'm afraid it might scare some of the children. Some children are frightened when they hear scary sounds. Do you have any other records at home that you think the other children would like to hear?"

In planning listening activities, the teacher might also carefully observe the type of music the children sing spontaneously. This gives a good clue to the kind of music they are accustomed to hearing, and such music may be a good starting point for initiating listening activities. In addition, teachers themselves need to listen to a variety of music. Although individual teachers may not enjoy a particular type of music, such as classical or folk, they should still listen to some of each type of music so that they can discuss it with the children.

Age Levels and Recordings

Children of all ages, from infancy on, enjoy and benefit from listening to recorded music. Recordings should be of good quality and in good condition so that children can begin developing discriminating ears. The recordings listed in this chapter are appropriate for all ages.

RECORDING CHILDREN

Another way to interest children in listening to music is to tape-record them, either individually or in groups. Children can be recorded singing, playing instruments, or just playing in the classroom. It is fun for children to guess whose voice they are hearing on the tape and thrilling when they hear their own. Because children have to listen very closely to identify voices on a tape, this activity facilitates the development of aural discrimination.

In addition to recording the children's voices, the teacher can record him- or herself or a parent singing or reading a story. The tape can be placed in the listening area where children can listen to it whenever they want. A picture book can accompany the tape so that the children can follow along.

Teachers can also record familiar sounds from outside or around the classroom. When the tape is played back, the children can try to guess what is making the sound. This activity also helps develop aural acuity.

LISTENING GAMES

There are a number of listening games that teachers can play with children to help them develop listening skills. These games usually focus on comparing sounds or identifying familiar sounds. For example, the teacher can drop two different-sounding objects and ask the children to compare the sound each makes when it hits the floor. Then the teacher can ask the children to cover their eyes and guess which one is dropped. The sounds of many combinations of objects can be compared—a nail and a pen, a rock and a pine cone, scissors and a pencil, a beanbag and a feather, and so on.

Two-year-olds usually need two easily distinguishable objects to choose between. Three- and four-year-olds may be able to choose among three objects. Older children can play the game using four or more objects.

In another listening game, the teacher can play a rhythm instrument and see if the children can identify it. A child might go behind a screen and play an instrument for the other children to guess. The sounds of the instruments can also be prerecorded.

Some interesting sound effect records are available. Children and adults alike may enjoy trying to identify the sounds on such records. Similar recordings can be made in the classroom by taping familiar sounds.

EXPERIMENTING WITH SOUND

Children learn about sound by experimenting with the sounds they can make with various objects. Teachers can foster the development of concepts on the nature of sound by giving children many opportunities to produce sounds and observe the outcome. The teacher might set aside a table or area of the room for experimenting with sound. There are many different sound concepts that could be explored. The teacher could suggest the following:

- Add water to various depths in a glass; tap the glass with a stick; observe how the amount of water affects the pitch.
- Hit a triangle with a wooden stick, a metal stick, a cotton swab, and a paper roll; compare the sounds.
- Drop beans into a can, a glass, a cardboard box, and a plastic bowl; compare the sounds.
- Compare the sounds of three triangles or drums of varying size.

LISTENING

The teacher might want to post a large sheet of paper in the experimenting area on which children could record or have the teacher record their impressions.

PAINTING AND WRITING TO MUSIC

Another way children can experience the feel of music is by painting as they listen to music. The children might wish to convey the mood of the music in their painting, or they might paint something representational to accompany the story or subject matter of the music. One three-year-old boy drew a beautiful, abstract painting of a "firebird" while listening to Stravinsky's *Firebird*. The teacher should let the children create whatever they like rather than limiting their imaginations by suggesting that they draw a particular thing.

Children may also enjoy writing a story to convey the way the music makes them feel. Preschool children could tell their story to a teacher, who could write it down; primary-age children could write down their own ideas.

LISTENING THROUGHOUT THE DAY

Some of the activities suggested in this chapter, such as the listening games, may be used as group activities; but most should be available for much of the day for children to investigate when they are interested. The teacher should carefully plan listening activities to have in the classroom. In addition, the extraneous sounds children make throughout the day should be pointed out and discussed. Children encounter many interesting sounds each day, but they may not notice these sounds unless the teacher draws attention to them. Some examples of sounds that teachers might want to point out to the children are:

- The difference between the sound of children's voices in their room and the sound of children's voices coming from other classrooms.
- The sound of the hammer when it hits the nail and when it hits the wood.
- The different sounds birds make.
- The sound of their feet on the pavement and in the grass, on the linoleum and on the carpet.
- The difference between the quick steps of children and the slower steps of adults.

The list of interesting sounds is infinite. The teacher should not only point out the sounds but also ask questions that encourage children to consider why things sound the way they do.

Many teachers, particularly in the preschool, use records as background music. This practice may actually *discourage* listening, since people tend to tune out sounds to which they are not actively attending. Listening to music can be encouraged by playing records when the children request them. The teacher can also suggest listening to a record as a specific activity.

SUMMARY Listening activities help children focus on sound, develop aural acuity, develop an awareness and understanding of sound, and enjoy music. Activities can include listening to guest performers, listening to a variety of recordings, hearing recordings of themselves, playing listening games, experimenting with sound, and painting or writing to music. Children's interest in listening is fostered when a quiet, comfortable area for listening is provided in the classroom. Children should be encouraged to listen to and explore the sounds around them throughout the day.

NOTES 1. "Tubby the Tuba," Disneyland record #1287 (1963).
2. "I Know an Old Lady Who Swallowed a Fly," from *Birds, Beasts, Bugs, and Little Fishes* (New York: Folkways Records and Service Corporation, 1968).

Berger, Melvin. *The Violin Book*. New York: Lothrop, Lee, and Shepard, 1972.

———. *The Clarinet and Saxophone Book*. New York: Lothrop, Lee, and Shepard, 1975.

Craig, Jean. *The Woodwinds*. Minneapolis: Lerner Publications, 1963.

Luttrell, Guy. *The Instruments of Music*. New York: Thomas Nelson, 1977.

Suggs, William W. *Meet the Orchestra*. New York: Macmillan, 1966.

Warren, Fred. *The Music of Africa*. Englewood Cliffs, N.J.: Prentice-Hall, 1970.

Weil, Lise. *Things That Go Bang*. New York: McGraw-Hill, 1969.

**SELECTED
BIBLIOGRAPHY**

7
Musical Concepts

LEARNING ABOUT some basic music concepts can help young children better understand both music and the nature of sound. In addition, since each of these concepts focuses on a particular aspect of sound, listening skills are strengthened. Three basic music concepts are appropriate to explore with young children: loud and soft, fast and slow, and high and low. As with all other areas of music, children will gain understanding of these concepts through actual experimentation with them.

LOUD AND SOFT

One of the first sound concepts children understand is loud and soft, or *dynamics.* Children form concepts of loud and soft by producing sounds and then listening to them. Gradually, over a long period of time, children make associations between the force they exert when striking an object and the resulting sound. They also make associations between the type of material used to produce a sound and the resulting sound, and between their distance from the sound and the volume of the sound.

Learning about Loud and Soft

Teachers can introduce loud and soft by playing loudly and then softly on an instrument. A nonpitched instrument such as a drum or wood block should be used so that the children do not confuse dynamics with pitch. (As with all concepts, it is important to isolate the concept being presented. Just as the teacher would not mix color with shape, so music concepts such as dynamics and pitch should not be mixed.) The teacher can begin by playing a drum loudly and asking the children how it sounds. The children can compare the sounds the teacher plays on the drum and each time decide whether it is loud and soft. The teacher can then invite each child to play something loud or soft on the drum while the other children listen. The teacher can help the children understand the concept of how loud and soft are produced by encouraging them to talk about and compare the way they hit the drum to get a loud sound with how they hit it to get a soft sound. Some unexpected ideas may surface. For example, when asked how she hit the drum to get a loud sound, one three-year-old girl answered that she hit it with her hand. When asked how she produced a soft sound, she replied, "With the other hand." Repeated experimentation is necessary before young children learn to associate the force applied to an instrument with the loudness of the resulting sound.

Experimenting with producing loud and soft sounds helps children understand what makes sounds loud or soft; their listening skills can also be sharpened by listening for loud and soft. The teacher can play or sing something and then ask the children whether it was loud or soft, or can ask a child to play something so that the other children can listen for loud and soft. Children can also listen for degrees of loudness or softness. The teacher can play two loud sounds and ask the children which was louder, or two soft sounds and ask the children which was softer. Making these finer discriminations helps children develop their aural acuity.

There are other ways to reinforce concepts of loud and soft. Children can sing a song loudly and then softly. They can play a loud accompaniment on rhythm instruments and then a soft accompaniment. In addition, movements can be associated with dynamics. The children can march around the room stamping loudly to loud music, then tiptoe to soft music. All these activities encourage children to listen and compare loud and soft music.

Once children can clearly hear the difference between

loud and soft and correctly label sounds as such, the teacher can point out that some sounds are neither loud nor soft, but somewhere in between. The same activities that were used to produce and listen for loud and soft sounds can now be used with the addition of medium-volume sounds. The children will thus be playing sounds that are loud, medium, and soft, and also listening for sounds in these three gradations. The addition of the medium-volume sound will encourage children to listen even more carefully to the gradations of sound volume they hear.

Other factors besides the force applied to an object affect the resulting sound. The material of the object being struck, as well as the type of device used to strike it, also affects the volume of sound, as does the distance between the sound and the listener. Once children have formed concepts about how the force with which they hit an object affects the volume of the sound, the teacher can encourage the children to experiment with other factors that affect the dynamics of sound.

Factors Affecting Dynamics

Children can perform many experiments that will help them discover how the type of material being struck affects the sound. For example, they can compare the sound of a hammer hitting wood with that of a hammer hitting hard foam. In addition, the teacher can make available a wide variety of materials for the children to strike with a beater and compare the dynamics: wood, paper, sponge, brick, plastic, hard foam, and so on. The teacher will need to help the children verbalize how hard they hit each object and how loud it sounded. For example:

Teacher: I barely heard anything when you hit the sponge. How hard did you hit it?
Child: I hit it hard.
Teacher: Now hit the brick hard and we'll listen for how loud it sounds.
Child: It sounded loud. The sponge sounded soft, but the brick sounded loud.

Children can also experiment with how different types of mallets affect dynamics. For example, they can play a drum with a wood mallet and then with a felt mallet, and listen for which is louder. Again, the teacher can help them verbalize the comparison. Encouraging children to put what they hear into words helps them formulate and remember these important concepts.

Children can also make discoveries about how distance affects sound volume. They can listen to the drum up close and then listen to it far away and compare the volume. They can also compare the sounds of nearby voices with the voices of people far away, and talk about how each sounds. Comparing distant sounds and nearby sounds again and again helps children become aware of how the distance factor affects the volume of sound.

Getting Louder, Getting Softer

Once children are accustomed to comparing sounds that are loud and soft, they may enjoy listening to music that **crescendos** (becomes gradually louder; pronounced cruh-SHEN-doe) and **decrescendos** (becomes gradually softer; pronounced DAY-cruh-SHEN-doe). A good recording for hearing crescendo is Grieg's "In the Hall of the Mountain King," from the *Peer Gynt Suite #1*. There is a steady crescendo throughout the entire piece.

Children may enjoy playing crescendos and decrescendos on their instruments. Again, it is best to start with a nonpitched instrument so that the children do not confuse pitch direction with volume direction.

As children listen to music getting louder and softer, the teacher and children can talk about how the crescendo or decrescendo affects the mood of the music. The children may wish to add some crescendos or decrescendos to the songs they sing. For example, in "Fire Truck Song" (Example 5.1) children may wish to add a gradual crescendo on the first two lines to recreate the sound of the approaching fire truck and a decrescendo on the last two lines to depict the fire truck getting farther and farther away.

Dynamics Throughout the Day

Teachers should call attention to loud and soft sounds throughout the day. For example, the clock ticking and water dripping are soft, but a chair scraping across the floor and the door slamming are loud. As the children interact with objects in the environment, the teacher can observe the sounds produced and talk to the children about how their actions affected the sound. Statements such as the following help children form concepts of loud and soft:

118

"You set that book down very carefully, and it barely made a sound. That was very soft."

"That puzzle hit the floor hard. It made a loud noise. When you set it down gently, the sound is very soft."

Teachers can also point out natural crescendos and decrescendos in the environment. The sound of the fire truck as it draws closer and then moves farther away is a natural crescendo, decrescendo. So is the sound of children's voices as they draw close and then move away. The sound of a jet coming near and then flying away is yet another example. Each time the teacher draws the child's attention to sounds such as these and labels them appropriately, concepts of loud and soft and crescendo and decrescendo are reinforced, and vocabulary is increased.

Age Levels and Dynamics

A child's age and stage of development will affect how loud and soft are perceived and how well they are understood. Infants and toddlers enjoy banging objects and listening to the sounds that are produced. Adults can increase children's vocabulary by labeling the corresponding sounds as loud or soft.

Two-Year-Olds

Two-year-olds may be able to label sounds as loud or soft without understanding what makes a sound loud or soft. For example, a two-year-old was taken by his parents to see fireworks on the Fourth of July. The loud sound of the fireworks frightened him, and he covered his ears. Several weeks later his parents again took him to see fireworks, but this time from a park some distance away from the place where the fireworks were set off. The parents explained that the fireworks would not be loud because they were far away. Nevertheless, as soon as he saw the first firework—even though he heard nothing—the little boy covered his ears. No amount of explanation on his parents' part could convince him to uncover his ears. They were fireworks, and therefore they were loud. His four-year-old brother, on the other hand, understood the reason that the fireworks would not be loud, and did not cover his ears.

Preschool Children

By the time children are three or four years old, if they are encouraged to experiment with sound and if adults talk to them about the sounds they produce, they begin to form concepts about why sounds are loud or soft. They may understand that hitting a drum hard makes a loud noise but may not yet realize that drums heard at a distance are soft because they are far away, not because of the way they are being played. Experimenting with sound and distance as suggested in this chapter will help children formulate these concepts. Exploring the volume of sound produced by hitting various materials is also appropriate.

Primary-Age Children

Most primary-age children are able to label sounds as loud, medium, or soft, and may also be able to hear crescendos and decrescendos; but they may be still formulating concepts about how various materials affect dynamics. Teachers can help primary-age children form these concepts by providing a variety of materials for experimentation. They can also encourage children to listen for fine gradations of volume and to apply dynamics to the songs they sing. In addition, teachers of primary children may wish to introduce the musical terms for dynamics:

- Loud—*forte* (pronounced FOR-tay).
- Soft—*piano* (pronounced pea-AH-no).
- Medium—*mezzo forte* (pronounced MET-zo FOR-tay).
- Becoming louder—*crescendo*.
- Becoming softer—*decrescendo*.

FAST AND SLOW

Another aspect of music that teachers can explore with young children is ***tempo***—how fast or slow the music is. As with listening for dynamics, listening for tempo improves children's listening skills and increases their understanding of music.

Learning about Fast and Slow

Teachers can introduce tempo in the same way that they introduced dynamics. First the teacher plays something fast on an instrument and asks the children if it sounds fast or slow. As with introducing dynamics, the teacher should use a non-pitched instrument so that the children do not confuse tempo with pitch. The teacher next plays something slow on the instrument so that the children can compare the fast and slow MUSICAL CONCEPTS

playing. Then the teacher can invite the children to play fast and slow on the instrument. Actually producing fast and slow sounds helps the children establish these concepts firmly in their minds.

Even trained musicians have to guard against a tendency to play fast music loudly and slow music softly. Teachers should be careful to play both fast and slow music at the same dynamic level so that the children do not confuse tempo with dynamics.

Children can listen for tempo in music. One of the best examples of alternating fast and slow tempos is Brahms's *Hungarian Dance #5*. Short, fast sections are followed by short, slow sections, with a marked contrast.

There are other activities that can reinforce concepts of tempo for young children. Children can sing a song fast and then sing it slowly. They may wish to decide on tempos for familiar songs. Perhaps they will want to sing a song about a turtle in a slow tempo since turtles move slowly, and a song about a rabbit in a fast tempo since rabbits hop quickly. Children can also coordinate their body movements with the tempo of the music—running to fast music and walking to slow music. Experiencing fast and slow with their whole bodies gives children more information on the real meaning of fast and slow. All these activities encourage the children to listen carefully for tempo in music.

Once the children have become adept at identifying fast and slow music, the teacher can point out that some music is neither fast nor slow, but at a medium speed. Children can be encouraged to play fast, medium, and slow tempos and to listen for these gradations of tempo in music. The addition of the medium tempo will encourage still more discriminating listening.

Speeding Up, Slowing Down

Once children have become adept at identifying tempo in music, they can be introduced to the concepts of *accelerando* (becoming gradually faster; pronounced ack-chel-ler-AHN-doe) and *decelerando* (becoming gradually slower; pronounced day-chel-ler-AHN-doe). The teacher can begin by playing something on a drum that starts slowly and gradually becomes faster. A drum or other nonpitched instrument is used so that the children do not confuse tempo changes with

121

pitch changes. The teacher can ask the children if the drum music was fast or slow; although some children may say fast because that is what they heard last, others may note that the music started slowly and then became fast. The teacher should repeat the example so that the children can listen again. Next the teacher can play something that starts fast and gradually becomes slower. The children and teacher can again discuss how the music sounded. Finally, interested children can play rhythms that start slowly and speed up, or start fast and slow down, while the other children listen. The teacher can suggest that the drum will be available in the classroom so that interested children can practice playing music that speeds up and slows down. Having an opportunity to experiment repeatedly with accelerando and decelerando reinforeces these concepts in the children's minds.

In addition to playing music that speeds up or slows down, children can listen to accelerando and decelerando in music. "In the Hall of the Mountain King," from Grieg's *Peer Gynt Suite #1*, which was used to demonstrate crescendo, is also a good example of accelerando. The entire piece gets gradually louder and faster until the end.

Children can perform movements to accompany accelerando and decelerando. For example, the teacher can use a drum to play a walking rhythm that gradually gets faster until the children are running, and then slows down again until they are walking. Children can also add accelerando and decelerando to the songs they sing. For instance, in "The Train" (Example 7.1) the children might want to pretend that the train is leaving the station and gradually getting faster and faster, and thus sing the song with an accelerando.

Tempo Throughout the Day

There are many examples of tempo in the children's environment, and the teacher can reinforce concepts of fast and slow by pointing these out whenever they occur. For example, the teacher might want to suggest that the children compare the sound of children's feet as they walk and run. A rainstorm provides an excellent example of tempo. The children can listen as the first raindrops fall, and continue to listen as the raindrops fall closer and closer together, creating a faster and faster tempo. The children will thus hear not only slow and fast tempos, but a natural acceleration as well. Another naturally occurring acceleration is the sound of a ball as it

Example 7.1
THE TRAIN

Ruth McConn Spencer

Choo, choo, choo, choo,   Choo, choo, choo, choo,

See the big long train, Oh!

Choo, choo, choo, choo,   Choo, choo, choo, choo,

Take me far a- way, Oh!

Source: Laura Bryant, *More Sentence Songs for Little Singers* (Cincinnati: Willis Music Company, 1939). Used by permission, Willis Music Co., Inc.

bounces. At first the bounces are far apart; but as the ball gets closer and closer to the ground, the bounces become closer and closer together, and the tempo increases. By pointing out these naturally occurring tempos, the teacher encourages the children to observe carefully and listen attentively to tempos and tempo changes, and reinforces these concepts in their minds.

Age Levels and Tempo
Toddlers

Toddlers begin to learn the words *fast* and *slow* if adults apply these terms to their actions. When the child runs, if the adult says, "You're running fast," the child begins to associate *fast* with running. If adults also apply the words *fast* and *slow* to moving objects in the child's environment, the child begins to generalize these terms to the speed of objects outside of him- or herself.

Adults can begin to apply the terms *slow* and *fast* to the music children hear. After singing a lullaby, the adult might say, "That was a slow song." Such statements encourage children to generalize the terms *fast* and *slow* to sounds that are heard as well as objects that are seen.

Preschool Children

Children ages three to five can begin to compare fast and slow tempos in music. Concepts of accelerando and decelerando may be more difficult for them to hear; but if they are encouraged to follow music that speeds up with body movements that speed up, or music that slows down with body movements that slow down, these concepts are more quickly absorbed.

Primary-Age Children

Children in the primary grades will almost certainly know what *fast* and *slow* mean, but they may not be accustomed to applying these terms to music. Thus the teacher will need to follow the same procedure in introducing tempo to primary-age children as would be used to introduce the concept to preschool children. First isolate fast and slow rhythms by playing them on a nonpitched instrument, then invite the children to create fast and slow music, and finally play music for listening that emphasizes fast and slow. Primary teachers should not introduce accelerando and decelerando until they are certain that the children can identify fast and slow tempos in the music. Teachers of primary-age children might want to apply the standard music terms for tempo:

- Slow—*andante* (pronounced ahn-DAHN-tay).
- Very slow—*largo* (pronounced LAR-go); *adagio* (pronounced a-DAH-zhee-oh).
- Moderate—*moderato* (pronounced mah-dur-AH-toe).
- Fast—*allegro* (pronounced uh-LAY-grow).
- Very fast—*presto* (pronounced PRESS-toe).
- Becoming faster—*accelerando*.
- Becoming slower—*decelerando*; *ritardando* (pronounced rih-tar-DAHN-doe).

HIGH AND LOW

A third musical concept that teachers can introduce to children is **pitch**—how high or low the music is. Pitch concepts are somewhat more abstract than dynamics or tempo and less easily related to concepts with which the children are familiar. Nevertheless, young children can perceive the difference between high sounds and low sounds once they have had sufficient practice creating and listening to high and low sounds. Listening for pitch not only improves listening skills but also greatly increases aural acuity.

Applying the terms *loud* and *soft* to music is easy to understand because we use those terms to refer to loud and soft sounds in our environment. Similarly, referring to music as fast or slow also seems logical because these terms relate to fast or slow speeds in the environment. Unfortunately, the terms *high* and *low*, applied to pitch, have no environmental corollary. High pitches are not physically higher than low pitches. (They are called *high* because they have a higher number of vibrations per second than low pitches do.) Nevertheless, children can learn to associate these terms with the appropriate pitch levels.

When introducing children to the terms *high* and *low* in music, it is helpful if the teacher encourages the children to move their hands either high or low according to the sound of the pitch. This helps the children make the association between the terms *high* and *low* and the sound of high and low pitches. The teacher begins by singing a high pitch and holding his or her hand high, then singing a low pitch and placing his or her hand down low. The terms *high* and *low* are applied to the corresponding pitches. At this point the children can be encouraged to sing and move their bodies along with the teacher. As they sing the high note, they reach up high and say *high*, and as they sing the low note, they reach down low and say *low*:

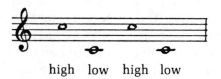

high   low   high   low

This activity or variations of it should be repeated on several subsequent days. In addition, the teacher can relate high and low to a pitched instrument. The teacher can demonstrate that the shortest bar on the xylophone sounds the highest, and the longest bar sounds the lowest. If the xylophone has removable bars, the teacher can at first put only the highest and lowest bars on the instrument, since it is easier for the children to discriminate first between pitches of greater contrast. Just as the children would first learn to differentiate between contrasting colors, such as red and blue, before learning to distinguish between more similar colors, such as red and orange, so children first learn to differentiate between pitches of sharper contrast before learning to distinguish between pitches more nearly alike. The xylophone can be left out in the classroom for the children to explore in relation to pitch. If there is a piano in the room, the teacher can also relate pitch to the piano keyboard.

Once children have learned to sing high and low pitches, the teacher can encourage them to listen for high and low in music. The teacher can explain that although all instruments have a range of high and low sounds, some instruments play much higher or lower than other instruments do. The teacher and children can compare the sounds of music played on the violin and on the string bass. They can also compare the trumpet and the tuba. It is preferable to compare similar instruments because the tone quality is similar and the children can concentrate on pitch. The violin and string bass are both string instruments and thus have a similar *timbre* (pronounced TAM–burr) or tone quality. The trumpet and tuba are both brass instruments. Comparing a very high instrument with a very low instrument, as in the foregoing examples, is easier for children than comparing two instruments that are closer together in pitch. These comparisons help them differentiate between high sounds and low sounds.

There are other activities that also emphasize pitch differences in music. If drums of various sizes are available, the children can compare the sounds and form concepts on how size affects pitch. The small drum, like the small bar on the xylophone, is highest in sound. Another activity that helps children learn about pitch is plucking the high and low strings on the autoharp or zither. The children can actually see that the high string vibrates more rapidly than the low string. Still another activity that encourages children to differentiate between high and low sounds incorporates body movement with listening for pitch. The children walk on tiptoe, stretching high, when they hear high music, and bend down and walk close to the floor when they hear low music. All these activities encourage children to listen carefully to high and low sounds, and help them form concepts about the nature of pitch in music.

By the time children have experimented many times with playing melody instruments and listening for pitch, they will probably realize that some pitches fall between the high tones and the low tones. As children become aware of the continuum of pitches, the teacher can introduce another music concept—pitch direction.

Going Up, Going Down

Any two consecutive pitches must do one of three things: go up, go down, or stay the same. Teachers can help the children hear whether the melody goes up, goes down, or stays the same.

The teacher can begin by playing two notes on the xylophone or singing two notes, and asking the children whether the second note was higher, lower, or the same. This game can be played several times, with the children showing the relationship between the pitches with their hands. At first the two notes should be far enough apart so that the children can easily tell whether the second note was higher, lower, or the same. Gradually, the teacher can make the pitches closer and closer together.

Once the children are accustomed to comparing the direction between two pitches, the teacher can play a short line of music that either goes up, goes down, or stays the same. The children can follow the direction of the music with their hands. A simple song like the one in Example 7.2 can help children listen for melodic direction.

Besides listening for melodic direction, singing examples of melodic direction, and diagraming melodic direction with their hands, children can also play melodies that go up, go down, or stay the same. On the xylophone the children can actually see as well as hear the pitch direction; this helps them associate the terms up (right), down (left), and same with what they hear.

Pitch Throughout the Day

There are some recognizable high and low sounds that we hear during the day, and children's concepts of high and low

Example 7.2
Going up and down the scale

We   are   go-   ing   up   the   scale,

Now   we're   go-   ing   down   the   scale,

And   we   stay   the   same.

sound are reinforced if the teacher points them out whenever they occur. For example, children can compare the chirping of birds with the barking of a dog and decide which animal has the higher voice. If several dogs are barking, children may even be able to determine which dog has the highest voice. An excellent example of a sound that gets higher and then lower is a siren, which gets steadily higher in pitch as it approaches and then lower in pitch as it moves farther away. Making pitch associations with these environmental sounds encourages children to listen carefully to the pitches of the sounds around them.

Age Levels and Pitch
Toddlers

Toddlers' voices normally do not have much range, so toddlers typically can not sing high and low pitches. They enjoy body movements, however, and can imitate the teacher stretching on the high notes and touching the floor on the low notes. The high-low example used in this chapter is thus appropriate for toddlers as well as for older children. Moving their bodies to high and low sounds helps even very young children begin to form concepts of pitch in music.

Preschool Children

Children ages three to five can begin to distinguish between high and low sounds in music if they are encouraged to sing and play high and low sounds, and to move their bodies to correspond to the sounds they hear. Hearing pitch direction, which requires much finer auditory discrimination, may be difficult for this age group. Even if the teacher decides not to introduce melodic direction formally to the class, it can still be pointed out to individual children as they play the xylophone or make up tunes.

Since many primary-age children have not yet been introduced to the concept of high and low sounds in music, primary teachers should follow the same procedure in introducing *high* and *low* as preschool teachers —— Sing high and low pitches while moving their arms high and low, play high and low on instruments, and listen to high and low in music. Pitch concepts take longer to formulate than do concepts of dynamics or tempo; but once the children are competent at hearing high and low pitches, primary teachers can begin exploring melodic direction with the children.

Primary-Age Children

SUMMARY

Learning about particular aspects of music encourages children to listen more discriminatingly and increases their understanding of sound and music. Teachers can introduce concepts of dynamics (loud and soft), tempo (fast and slow), and pitch (high and low). Children need to explore each of these areas concretely—by singing, experimenting with instruments, and moving their bodies in concordance with the sounds they hear. In addition, children can be encouraged to listen for dynamics, tempo, and pitch in music, and to incorporate these concepts into their own singing. Finally, teachers can reinforce these concepts by pointing them out to children in the sounds they hear throughout the day.

SELECTED BIBLIOGRAPHY

Choate, Robert A.; Kjelson, Lee; Berg, Richard C.; and Troth, Eugene W. *Introducing Music*. New Dimensions in Music. New York: American Book Company, 1970.

Findlay, Elsa. *Rhythm and Movement, Applications of Dalcroze Eurhythmics*. Evanston, Ill.: Summy-Birchard Company, 1971.

Funes, Donald J., and Munson, Kenneth. *Musical Involvement: A Guide to Perceptive Listening*. New York: Harcourt Brace Jovanovich, 1975. (Book and set of recordings).

8
Orff Concepts with Young Children

CARL ORFF (1895–1982) was a well-known German composer and music educator. He began giving music lessons to children in the 1930s and out of this experience evolved his own method of music instruction. He also designed a complete set of instruments for young children. The Orff method of music instruction has become very popular in both Europe and the United States.

The Orff method is designed to help children grow not only musically, but in many other ways as well. First of all, it provides a natural outlet for the energy of young children. In addition, it is intellectually stimulating and thus fosters cognitive growth. The Orff system is designed to accommodate a wide range of developmental levels simultaneously and thereby to encourage cooperation among groups of children. Fine-motor skills are developed as the children perform on the instruments. Finally, the method encourages children to listen to sounds and create tonal beauty.[1]

The Orff method is based on the actual performance of music by young children. To facilitate young children's ability to create music on instruments, Orff designed a series of instruments specifically sized for children. These include a number of percussion instruments and a variety of melody instruments. The latter include xylophones, glockenspiels, and metallophones, all with removable bars. The xylophones have wooden bars and come in three sizes: soprano (high-pitched; alto (medium-pitched); and bass (low-pitched; pronounced BASE). The glockenspeils have metal bars, are smaller than xylophones, and are sized soprano and alto. The metallophones have metal bars that continue to resonate for a longer period of time after being struck than do those of xylophones and glockenspiels. Metallophones also come in two sizes: soprano and alto. The Orff instruments are all of high quality, and each has a lovely tone.

The Orff method is a detailed and comprehensive approach to music instruction. For the purposes of this book, only those aspects of the Orff system that can readily be incorporated for classroom use by teachers who are nonmusicians are included. Three areas will be considered: rhythmic activities, melodic activities, and creativity.

RHYTHMIC ACTIVITIES

Orff formulated a number of activities to help children develop rhythmic skills. Speech exercises and echo clapping, as used by Orff, were discussed in Chapter 3. In addition, rhythmic ostinati can be used to develop rhythmic and listening skills in young children. An *ostinato* (pronounced AHS-tih-NAH-toe; plural, *ostinati* —AHS-tih-NAH-tee) is a repeated pattern; therefore, a *rhythmic ostinato* is a repeated rhythmic pattern. Ostinati can range from very simple, such as clapping a steady beat, to long and complex. They can be clapped or played on rhythm instruments, and can be used to accompany speech exercises or songs or in combination with other rhythmic ostinati. Performing ostinati helps children develop listening and cognitive skills as well as rhythmic awareness, since they must aurally separate the repeated pattern from the rhythm of the song.

Speech Patterns with Rhythmic Ostinati

Rhythmic ostinati can be used to accompany familiar chants or speech patterns. The first pattern introduced should be the steady beat of the chant so that the children can relate other patterns to the beat[2]. The children may start by clapping the beats of the chant "Rain, Rain Go Away" (Example 4.1):

Next the children could try clapping twice per beat, with the first clap coming on the beat and the second clap coming halfway between the first beat and the second beat. (The symbol ⊓ is used to represent this. The vertical stroke on the left is the basic beat, the vertical stroke on the right is the sound occurring midway between the previous beat and the next beat.[2]

TAPE

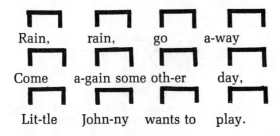

A slightly more complicated pattern would involve having the children clap once on the first beat and twice on the second beat. The ostinato, therefore, is a two-beat pattern; that is, the figure ⌐⊓ repeats itself every two beats. The challenging part of this ostinato is the contrast created when two claps fall on a one-syllable word and one clap falls on a two-syllable word:

TAPE

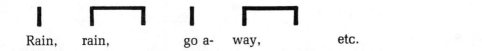

This pattern could be reversed to create the following ostinato:

When children are accustomed to clapping an ostinato while they say a chant, ostinati involving a combination of clapping and knee slapping (patting the lap with both hands) can be started. Examples 8.1–8.4 show how the same ostinati previously presented can be made more challenging by alternating clapping and knee slapping. Many combinations are possible.

Example 8.1
RAIN, RAIN, GO AWAY

Traditional

Clapping

Knee slapping

Rain,   rain,   go a-   way,   etc.

Example 8.2
RAIN, RAIN, GO AWAY

Traditional

Clapping

Knee slapping

Rain,   rain,   go   a- way,   etc.

The clap comes on each beat and
the knee slap comes in between the beats.

Example 8.3
RAIN, RAIN, GO AWAY

Traditional

Clapping

Knee slapping

Rain,   rain,   go   a- way,   etc.

Clap twice on the first beat,
slap the knee twice on the second beat,
and then repeat the pattern.

Example 8.4
RAIN, RAIN, GO AWAY

Traditional

Clapping

Knee slapping

Rain,   rain,   go   a- way,   etc.

Clap on every beat,
slap the knee in between the first and second beat,
but not after the second beat.

Combination ostinati such as those in Examples 8.1–8.4 require strong concentration, well-developed listening skills, and rhythmic independence. For children who become proficient at performing clapping and knee slapping ostinati, a third motion can be added—stamping. Now the children must remember ostinati that involve clapping, knee slapping, and stamping. Needless to say, these more complex ostinati further develop memory, listening skills, and rhythmic independence. Examples 8.5–8.7 show some ostinati involving clapping, knee slapping, and stamping.

For advanced children, Orff adds yet another motion—finger snapping. This makes the ostinati even more challenging to remember and execute.

As soon as the children understand the concept of the ostinato, they should be encouraged to create their own. This fosters creativity as the children acquire rhythmic skills.

Speech exercises can also be accompanied by ostinati performed on rhythm instruments. The same patterns used for

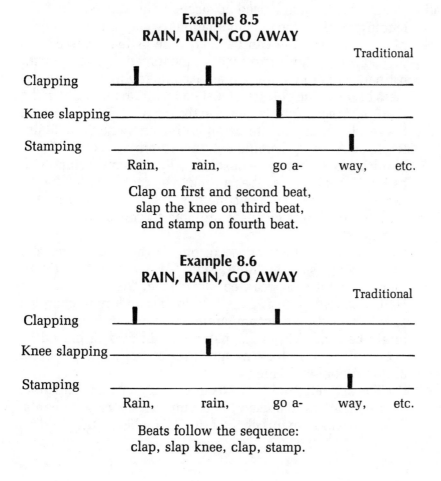

Example 8.5
RAIN, RAIN, GO AWAY

Traditional

Clapping

Knee slapping

Stamping

Rain,   rain,   go a-   way,   etc.

Clap on first and second beat,
slap the knee on third beat,
and stamp on fourth beat.

Example 8.6
RAIN, RAIN, GO AWAY

Traditional

Clapping

Knee slapping

Stamping

Rain,   rain,   go a-   way,   etc.

Beats follow the sequence:
clap, slap knee, clap, stamp.

135

Example 8.7
RAIN, RAIN, GO AWAY

Traditional

Beats follow the sequence:
clap twice, slap knee, clap twice, stamp.

clapping can be used, plus many more that teachers and children invent.

Songs with Rhythmic Ostinati

Rhythmic ostinati can be used to accompany songs in the same way they are used to accompany chants. Ostinati employing clapping or combinations of clapping, knee slapping, and stamping can be used. The ostinati can also be played on rhythm instruments. Accompanying songs with ostinati is more complex than accompanying speech exercises because the children must concentrate not only on the rhythm of the words, but also on the melody. For this reason, the teacher may wish to begin with a *chant* such as "Rain, Rain, Go Away" (Example 8.8; see Example 4.1), which the children are already accustomed to accompanying with ostinati, and then use it as a *song* to be accompanied by the same ostinati. Since this song has only three pitches, it is easy to sing; thus children are able to concentrate on the rhythm.

When the children are accustomed to accompanying very simple songs such as "Rain, Rain, Go Away" with ostinati, more difficult songs can be introduced. "Rain, Snow, and Hail" (Example 4.3) is a slightly longer and more complex song. The ostinato accompaniment shown in Example 8.9 might be used. This same pattern could also be played by some children on like rhythm instruments while the other children clap and sing.

The ostinati used in the examples are meant to illustrate how ostinati can be used to accompany songs and chants. As stated earlier in this chapter, it is desirable for the children to create the ostinati themselves since the Orff method is designed to develop creativity along with other musical skills.

Rhythmic ostinati can also be performed in combination, so that two or more patterns are played simultaneously. The class is divided into two or more groups, with each group

Combinations of Ostinati

Example 8.8
RAIN, RAIN, GO AWAY
Clap twice on first beat
and once on the second beat.

Traditional

Clapping

Rain, rain, go a-way, Come a-gain some oth-er day,

Lit-tle John-ny wants to play.

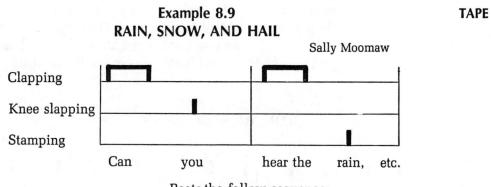

Example 8.9   TAPE
RAIN, SNOW, AND HAIL

Sally Moomaw

Clapping		
Knee slapping		
Stamping		

Can   you   hear the   rain,   etc.

Beats the follow sequence:
clap twice, slap knee, clap twice, stamp.

Copyright ©1978, 1980 by Sally Coup Moomaw.   **137** developing and performing its own ostinato. Performing two or more ostinati simultaneously requires even more concentration and independence of thought than performing one does, so the teacher should begin simply, with two easy ostinati. (Later the children can create their own more complex patterns.) Using the familiar example of "Rain, Rain, Go Away," one group of children can begin by clapping the beats. Then a second group can join in, clapping twice as fast. Finally, the chant can be added, accompanied by the two ostinati (see Example 8.10).

When the children are comfortable clapping the two different ostinati, two different rhythm instruments can be used to play the patterns. Having a different instrument on each pattern—for example, a triangle with group I and a wood block with group II—makes it easier for the children to separate the two different patterns aurally. When performing ostinati on rhythm instruments, it may be preferable to have small groups of about five children play the patterns on the instruments, since it is difficult to keep larger groups together.

Once the children are adept at performing two ostinati simultaneously, a third can be added. This third pattern might be half the speed of the beat. Again the group clapping the beat should start, followed by the second group clapping the faster notes, then the third group clapping the slower notes, and finally the chant. Instruments can be added later when the children are comfortable clapping the three patterns (see Example 8.11).

Songs can also be accompanied by two or more ostinati. As with accompanying chants, the group playing the beats begins, followed by each remaining group in succession, and finally by the addition of the song (Example 8.12; Example 2.19 for full song and text). Even after the class has become more advanced and each group is developing its own

Example 8.10
RAIN, RAIN, GO AWAY

Traditional

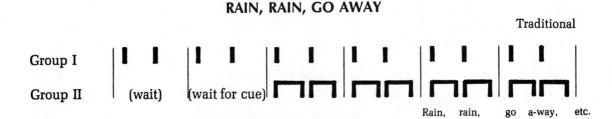

Example 8.11
RAIN, RAIN, GO AWAY

Traditional

Group I

Group II   (wait)   (wait for cue)

Group III   (wait)   (wait)   (wait)   (wait for cue)

Group I

Group II

Group III   rest   rest   rest   rest

Rain, rain, go a-way, etc.

ostinato, the teacher should still begin with one group and add each additional group in succession so that the children can clearly hear the pattern of each group. This also helps the groups stay together.

It is difficult to affix ages to Orff concepts since the abilities of individual children vary so widely. The sequence of presentation is of more concern than the ages of the children, and the teacher should follow the same sequence regardless of age. Although older children may move through the sequence of activities more rapidly than younger children do and may advance to more difficult activities, it is important

Presenting Rhythmic Ostinati

Example 8.12
SNOWFLAKES

TAPE

Nina M. Kenagy
Francis M. Arnold

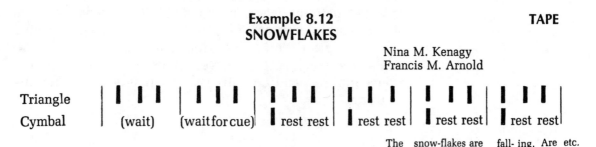

Triangle

Cymbal   (wait)   (wait for cue)   rest rest   rest rest   rest rest   rest rest

The snow-flakes are fall-ing, Are etc.

Source: Nina M. Kenagy and Francis M. Arnold, *Musical Experiences of Little Children* (Cincinnati: Willis Music Company, 1932). Used by permission, Willis Music Co., Inc.

to build on the fundamental patterns and gradually work toward increasingly complex goals.

The first ostinati should be short and simple and should be clapped. The children should begin by clapping the beats and move to more complicated patterns only when their feel for the beat is firmly established. Typically, some three-year-olds and many four-year-olds can clap on the beat. Children can begin playing ostinati on instruments once they are secure in clapping them.

Orff suggests that once children are accustomed to clapping ostinati, stamping should be added.[3] It is probably better, however, if knee slapping is added after clapping rather than stamping. Knee slapping is the same basic motion as clapping and is therefore easier for the children than stamping. It provides a more gradual transition from the simpler clapping to the more difficult clapping and stamping. Stamping can be added once the children grow accustomed to combining clapping and knee slapping.

Children can begin clapping ostinati to accompany songs once they are accustomed to performing ostinati with chants. Later two ostinati can be performed together to accompany chants and then songs.

Ostinati move gradually from simple to complex on several levels. First, the ostinati themselves are initially short and simple and become gradually longer and more complex rhythmically. Second, ostinati become progressively more complex as knee slapping and stamping are introduced. Finally, higher levels of complexity are achieved when two or more ostinati are performed simultaneously.

Children at various levels of development can cooperate in performing pieces accompanied by rhythmic ostinati. Younger or less advanced children can play the less complicated patterns, such as the steady beat; older or more advanced children can play and create more complicated patterns. In addition to fostering group cooperation, working with rhythmic ostinati develops listening skills, memory, concentration, and cognitive skills. It is also fun for the children.

MELODIC ACTIVITIES A second component of the Orff system involves accompanying songs with melodic ostinati. Melodic ostinati are similar to rhythmic ostinati—they are repeated melodic patterns. The melodic pattern is usually associated with a repeated rhythmic pattern; therefore, melodic ostinati are used to accompany songs in much the same way as are rhythmic ostinati.

The songs and ostinato accompaniments used in the Orff system are based on pentatonic scales. A *pentatonic scale* is a type of five-note scale wherein any two notes of the scale, played together, sound harmonious (see the Glossary for a more detailed definition). Therefore, if the children sing a song based on a pentatonic scale, any melodic ostinato based on that same scale that they use to accompany the song will work.

It may now be apparent why Orff designed his melody instruments (xylophones, glockenspiels, and metallophones) with removable bars. When the bars labeled F and B are removed, the instruments are set to a pentatonic scale. This makes it simple for even very young children to play pentatonic accompaniments.[4]

Selecting Pentatonic Songs

In order for the children to accompany songs with melodic ostinati, the songs as well as the instruments must be pentatonic. It is beyond the scope of this book to give instructions on how to determine whether a song is pentatonic. A listing of all the pentatonic songs in this book is at the end of this chapter.

Teachers can compose their own pentatonic songs by using the Orff-style melodic instruments. The teacher should first select the text for the song by either composing the words or using the words to a preexisting song or poem. Next the melodic instrument should be set to a pentatonic scale by removing the F and B bars. The teacher can then play melodies on the instrument until one is found that fits the words. Since the instrument has already been adjusted to play a pentatonic scale, the teacher can be sure that the resulting song will be pentatonic. Children can compose songs in the same way.

Accompanying Songs with Melodic Ostinati

The approach to accompanying a song with melodic ostinati is much the same as that for accompanying a song with rhythmic ostinati, except that now the song must be pentatonic. First the children need to be very familiar with the song so that they can sing it easily. Then a very simple ostinato can be introduced—at first, just a single note on the beat. The teacher can ensure that the child playing the ostinato plays the correct note by removing the other bars. The teacher should first start the child playing the ostinato and then begin the singing (see Example 8.13; for full song and text, see Example 2.14). Later a second ostinato can be added. Again, the child playing the beat begins, followed by the child playing the second ostinato, and finally by the singing (see Example 8.14).

TAPE

Example 8.13
IT WAS SNOW

Sally Moomaw

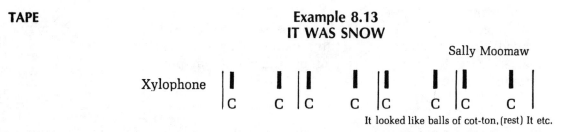

It looked like balls of cot-ton, (rest) It etc.

Example 8.14
IT WAS SNOW

Sally Moomaw

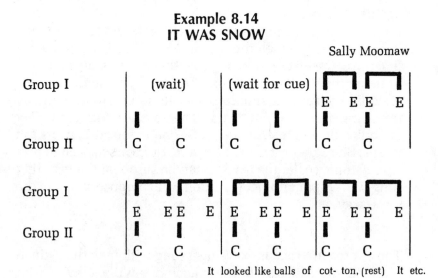

It looked like balls of cot- ton, (rest) It etc.

As the children become more advanced, a third ostinato can be added. Nevertheless, the song is always begun with the child playing the beat, followed by each successive ostinato and finally by the singing.

All these patterns are relatively simple. As the children become more advanced, however, they can begin to create their own patterns, which may be more difficult. The less advanced children can play the easier patterns. Note that in Examples 8.15 and 8.16 the song has one simple ostinato and two more difficult ones for accompaniment. "I Saw a Little Squirrel" (Example 8.17; see Example 2.23) is another song that can be accompanied by melodic ostinati.

Performing and listening to melodic ostinati help children aurally separate the various lines of music in a piece, especially if the ostinati are performed on instruments with different tone qualities. Along with listening skills, concentration and memory are developed as the children focus on each line. Fine-motor skills are also developed as the children play the instruments.

Example 8.15
IT WAS SNOW

Sally Moomaw

It looked like balls of cot-ton,(rest) It etc.

Example 8.16
IT WAS SNOW

Sally Moomaw

Group I	(wait)	(wait)	(wait)	(wait for cue)
Group II	(wait)	(wait for cue)	C D	E D
Group III	C C	C C	C C	C C

Group I	G AG E	G AG E	G AG E	G AG E
Group II	C D	E D	C D	E D
Group III	C C	C C	C C	C C

It looked like balls of cot- ton,(rest)   It etc.

Example 8.17
I SAW A LITTLE SQUIRREL

Sally Moomaw

Group I	(wait)	(wait for cue)
Group II	(wait)	E EE EE EE E
Group III	C C C C	C C C C

Group I	A GE GA GE G	A GE GA GE G
Group II	E EE EE EE E	E EE EE EE E
Group III	C C C C	C C C C

I   saw a lit- tle squir-rel,(rest) It etc.

Melodic ostinati are appropriate for children from the pre-school years through adulthood, since ostinati range in difficulty from very simple to long and complex. Once children are able to clap a steady beat, they can begin playing ostinati on the beat. Many three- and four-year-olds and most five-year-olds can do this. Gradually, the children can be encouraged to create longer and more difficult patterns. One of the most exciting aspects of the Orff system is that children on so many different developmental levels can cooperate to create music, with the less advanced children playing the simple patterns and the more advanced children playing the more difficult ones.

Age Levels and Melodic Ostinati

Children can compose lovely melodies and accompaniments with the Orff instruments. If the instruments are set to a pentatonic scale, two children can create melodies together; whatever they play will sound harmonious. In addition, children can compose melodies to fit words or improvise melodies over ostinati.

CREATING SONGS WITH ORFF INSTRUMENTS

Children can begin composing melodies by creating tunes to fit words or phrases. Creating a song to fit their own names is a good beginning activity. Children can begin by saying their names and then clapping the rhythm of the name. The rhythm can then be transferred to the melody instrument and melody thereby created to fit it (Example 8.18). Later, longer phrases or chants can form the basis for creating melodies

Creating Melodies to Fit Words

Example 8.18
Fitting a melody to a name

Beats								
Name	Em-i-	ly	Par-	ker,	Em-i-	ly	Par-	ker
Melody created	A A	G	E	D	C C D	E	G	

145

Example 8.19
Fitting a melody to a phrase

Beats									
Phrase	Let	me	tell you my		friends (silence). Ra-	chel	and Claire.		

Melody created	C	D	E	E G	A		G	D	E	C
						rest				
Accompanying ostinato	C	D	E	D	C	D	E	D		C

(Example 8.19). Once a child has learned to play the melody he or she has composed, another child might wish to play an ostinato to accompany it.

Improvising Melodies over Ostinati   Children can also create extemporaneous melodies over ostinati. The activity begins with one child playing the beat. Then other ostinati are added one at a time. Finally, one child creates a melody over the ostinati (Example 8.20).

Example 8.20
Extemporaneous melody over ostinati

Ostinati

(wait for cue)

G G G G | G G G G | G G G G | G G G G

(wait) (wait for cue)

E D DC D | E D DC D | E D DC D

C C C C | C C C C | C C C C | C C C C | C C C C

Melody created

C D EG AG | A C DEDC | etc.

Many Orff activities are suitable for performing in large groups. Other activities, however, are best performed individually or in small groups. For this reason, Orff instruments should be available for children to use throughout the day.

Melodic ostinati are best performed in small groups since only a few children can play the instruments at a time. If the instruments are available in the classroom, small groups of interested children can assemble, and the teacher can help them create melodies and accompaniments. Individual children can also compose songs and experiment with the instruments. The children may enjoy learning how to write down their songs and accompaniments using musical notation.

SUMMARY

Although originally conceived as a method of music instruction, the Orff system meets many developmental needs of young children. It encourages children to explore the various components of music actively and creatively as they create and perform rhythms and melodies on a variety of instruments. Such actual participation in the process of creating and producing music enables children to form concepts of how sound is produced, how music is created, and the difference between chaotic and organized sound. This furthers the cognitive development of young children.

Development is fostered in many other areas through the use of Orff's ideas. Listening skills are sharpened as children focus on various aspects of the music. For instance, speech exercises and rhythmic ostinati encourage children to listen specifically for rhythm, a skill that carries over to language development as children begin to break down words and sound them out. As children begin to compose and combine ostinati, they are encouraged to listen to more than one line of music—to hear more than just the melody. Children thus begin to hear music not only as a whole, but also as its individual components.

Another area of development that is improved through Orff activities is concentration and memory. It takes sharply focused attention to remember and repeat a pattern, whether rhythmic or melodic, especially when the pattern is used to accompany another line of music. As children progress through more difficult patterns, their concentration and memory skills develop concurrently.

Other areas that are developed through Orff experiences are fine-motor skills and group cooperation. Playing the rhythm and percussion instruments requires good eye-hand coordination, and this skill increases as children begin to create longer patterns and maneuver among more bars on the melodic instruments. Group cooperation, of course, is essential when children combine to produce an organized musical experience.

Preschool and primary teachers can use parts of the Orff method by developing activities based on rhythmic and melodic ostinati. The children can perform speech exercises and chants and can accompany them with ostinati involving clapping, knee slapping, and stamping, or using instruments. Songs can also be accompanied by rhythmic ostinati or by ostinati performed on melody instruments set to a pentatonic scale. At first the ostinati should by simple — clapping on the beat or playing a single note on the beat. Gradually, as the children develop a feel for rhythm, they should be encouraged to create their own patterns for accompaniment. As the children continue to develop, patterns can be combined. The essential component of the entire system is the children's involvement in creating music and in the music-making process. This is the key to developing real understanding of the nature of music in young children, as well as an incentive for young children to express themselves and develop their creativity musically.

SONGS IN THIS BOOK COMPATIBLE WITH PENTATONIC ACCOMPANIMENTS

Chapter 2

■ "Thunder" (Example 2.4)
■ "It Was Snow" (Example 2.14)
■ "I Saw a Little Squirrel" (Example 2.23)

Chapter 4

■ "Rain, Rain, Go Away" (Example 4.1)
■ "Rain, Snow, and Hail" (Example 4.3)
■ "Wind Song" (Example 4.4)

Chapter 5

■ "Step and Clap" (Example 5.7)
■ "A Gust of Fall Wind" (Example 5.8)

Chapter 10

■ "Where is Jeffrey?" (Example 10.2)
■ "Two Shoes" (Example 10.4)
■ "The Elephant" (Example 10.7)

NOTES

1. Carl Orff and Gunild Keetman, *Music for Children*, Vol. I, English version adapted by Margaret Murray (London: Schott and Company, 1958), Introduction.
2. Note that if note heads are added to this notation, the vertical stroke | becomes ♩ a quarter note—and the symbol ⊓ becomes ♫ eighth notes. Thus the notation used here is only one step removed from actual musical notation.
3. Orff and Keetman, *Music for Children*, p. 142.
4. Removing the F and B bars creates a pentatonic scale in the key of C. Other possibilities are removing the E and B bars—key of F, and removing the C and F bars—key of G.

SELECTED BIBLIOGRAPHY

Carley, Isabel McNeill. *Orff Re-Echoes*. American Orff—Schulwerk Association, 1977.

Keetman, Gunild. *Elementaria*. London: Schott and Company, 1970

Keller, Wilhelm. *Introduction to Music for Children*, English translation by Susan Kennedy. New York: Schott and Company, 1974.

Orff, Carl, and Keetman, Gunild. *Music for Children*, Vol. 1, English version by Margaret Murray. London: Schott and Company, 1958.

Orff-Schulwerk. *Nursery Rhymes and Songs*, English adaption by Doreen Hall. New York: Schott and Company, 1961.

——. *Eight English Nursery Songs*, English adaptation by Margaret Murray. London: Schott and Company, 1963a.

——. *Singing Games and Songs*, English adaptation by Doreen Hall. New York: Schott and Company, 1963b.

9

Music and the Exceptional Child

IN RECENT YEARS it has become increasingly common for handicapped children to be integrated into classrooms of nonhandicapped children at all levels, from preschool through high school. This so-called *mainstreaming* means that many preschool and primary teachers now have the opportunity to work with exceptional children as well as normal children. In addition, many teachers have gifted or talented children in their classes. Teachers need to give special consideration to the exceptional children in the class when preparing music experiences.

In this chapter, eight types of exceptional children are considered: (1) gifted and talented, (2) orthopedically handicapped, (3) learning-disabled, (4) emotionally disturbed, (5) hearing-impaired, (6) mentally retarded, (7) visually impaired, and (8) speech- and/or language-impaired. Each section discusses characteristics of the exceptionality, ways in which music can help the exceptional child develop, and modifications the teacher may need to consider when planning music activities for each type of exceptionality. Although this chapter considers exceptional children primarily in terms of mainstreamed classrooms, the same information would apply to exceptional children in homogeneous classrooms.

GIFTED AND TALENTED CHILDREN

Gifted and talented children are those with outstanding abilities that make them capable of high achievement. They include children with exceptional ability in any of the following areas:

- General intellectual ability.
- Specific academic aptitude.
- Creative or productive thinking.
- Leadership ability.
- Visual and performing arts abilities.
- Psychomotor ability.[1]

Music and Gifted and Talented Children

Music offers unique opportunities for gifted or talented children to expand their horizons and express themselves. Both creativity and cognitive growth can be enhanced through carefully planned music activities. A number of music activities focus on creative development. First, gifted children can be encouraged to compose their own songs and rhythms. This is a desirable activity for all of the children, but some children may be exceptionally talented in this area. Many opportunities should be provided for such talented children to develop their creative abilities.

Another area in which gifted and talented children can expand their creative talents is in developing movements to accompany music. Some groups may wish to choreograph a story or piece of music and make a production out of it. For example, in one preschool class, a group of talented children, under teacher guidance, wrote and produced their own television show based on a "Star Wars" theme. Part of the production included selecting, creating, and recording background music.[2] Yet another way in which talented children can be encouraged to develop their creativity is in adding words to existing songs. The teacher should allow for as much input from the children as possible.

Music can also further the cognitive development of gifted children. For these children, the teacher may wish to delve more deeply into music concepts and the physical properties of sound. Although experimenting with sound should be an important part of the curriculum for all the children, gifted children may wish to explore this area in more detail. The teacher should make the opportunity for such experimentation available and encourage children's activities. Some

152

gifted children may wish to begin notating music. The teacher could place a flannel board with a staff next to the xylophone and show the child where the note corresponding to each bar of the xylophone is located on the staff. In addition, gifted or talented children may be interested in learning to recognize a large number of musical instruments by sight and sound. Finally, gifted children can be challenged cognitively by creating and performing more complex Orff ostinati to accompany music.

Planning Music Activities for the Gifted or Talented Child

When planning for music groups, the teacher should include some activities that challenge the gifted or talented children in the class. This might include more complicated ostinati for them to perform, or it might involve encouraging them to create movements or words to fit songs. Multilevel activities, such as accompanying songs with several ostinati of varying difficulty, are appropriate since children at varying levels of development can perform together. Creative movement activities also allow children to become involved at their own levels of development. Painting or writing stories to music is another area in which children of differing ages or abilities can participate in the same activity at different levels.

The teacher should also plan activities that encourage gifted or talented children to develop their creativity. If some children are interested in composing songs, the teacher can record the songs for all the children to hear. The teacher can also generate ideas for the subject matter of songs or music. For example, in the class that produced the television show, the teacher discussed with the children what type of music they wished to use for the show, and provided them with instruments. The children then created the music. A teacher who notices particular musical talent in a child should let the child's parents know about it. The teacher may be able to suggest ways for the parents to help their child develop musically, perhaps by going to concerts or by taking music lessons. The teacher cannot assume that the creativity of talented children will continue to develop in an unstimulating environment. Rather, it is the teacher's responsibility to create a classroom environment in which gifted children are stimulated and encouraged to develop their creative talents.

Children with orthopedic handicaps have conditions that limit or prohibit the development of certain parts of their bodies. These conditions may be congenital or may result from accidents or disease. Orthopedic handicaps include spina bifida,[3] loss or deformity of limbs, severe burns, and cerebral palsy.[4] Children with orthopedic handicaps may exhibit some of the following behaviors:

- Impeded development of gross-motor functions.
- Delayed development because of frequent medical problems.
- Late speech and language problems (cerebral palsy).
- Fine-motor difficulty.
- Balance problems.
- Cognitive delay because ability to explore environment has been impeded.
- Memory problems (cerebral palsy).
- Poor eye-hand coordination.
- Listening problems (cerebral palsy).
- Concentration problems (cerebral palsy).
- Speech problems (cerebral palsy).[5]

Music and Children with Orthopedic Handicaps

Music activities can help orthopedically handicapped children develop in a number of ways. First, participation in the music group gives the orthopedically handicapped child a chance to join in and cooperate with other children. This encourages social development in both the handicapped child and the nonhandicapped children. The orthopedically handicapped child is able to participate in many music activities in exactly the same way as the nonhandicapped children. Other activities can be modified so that the orthopedically handicapped child can also participate.

Music activities also help the orthopedically handicapped child develop gross-motor skills. Rhythm and movement activities encourage the child to respond physically, and this helps develop those parts of the body that the child is capable of using. Such activities help develop muscle tone, balance, and coordination; they also encourage the orthopedically handicapped child to be more physically active.

The orthopedically handicapped child also benefits from music experiences in developing listening skills and sound discrimination. Singing, performing rhythmic activities, playing listening games, following movement songs with directions, listening for particular aspects of music, and playing and listening to instruments all encourage the child to focus on sound and listen for sound differentiations. This aids in the development of listening skills.

Speech and language development are also encouraged by music activities. Singing songs encourages children to use their speech, and songs and chants can be selected that emphasize speech sounds that the orthopedically handicapped child is working on. The language used in the songs and rhythm activities and the directions given by the teacher can also expand the vocabulary of both the orthopedically handicapped child and the rest of the class.

Another area in which music activities can help the orthopedically handicapped child develop is fine-motor skills and eye-hand coordination. Clapping activities, instrument playing, and finger plays all foster growth in this area.

Cognitive development can also be furthered in orthopedically handicapped children by music activities. Many of these children have had limited opportunities to explore their environment because of the nature of their handicap and the need for frequent medical attention. Experimenting with using their voices in singing, experiencing rhythms with their bodies, and exploring a variety of instruments can help orthopedically handicapped children develop important cognitive concepts.

Finally, music activities can help orthopedically handicapped children develop concentration and memory. Music activities encourage children to focus attention; children develop concentration as they listen to the words of songs, the sounds of rhythms and instruments, and the directions for movement.

Planning Music Activities for the Orthopedically Handicapped Child

Orthopedically handicapped children can participate in most music activities if some modifications are made to accommodate them. It is crucial for the teacher to select a position for the child which makes him or her feel balanced and comfortable and allows the child maximum freedom to see and move. Some children may feel most comfortable lying on the floor with a bolster under their chests to give them support and free their arms, hands, and head for movement. Other children prefer to sit as the other children do, since this makes them feel more a part of the group. An adult can create an excellent seating arrangement by sitting with legs crossed to make a well with the legs in which the orthopedically handicapped child can sit. Some children may be comfortable in a chair with arms on each side for support and the legs removed so that the child is sitting on the same level as the other children. All these positions provide balance and support for the child while allowing for as much movement as possible.[6] In addition, an adult should be seated near the orthopedically handicapped child to observe the child and make sure he or she is comfortable and balanced throughout the group activity period.

Orthopedically handicapped children enjoy and benefit from singing experiences. Songs that use each child's name or allow each child to contribute to the song, such as telling what they are wearing, build positive self-concepts and make everyone feel part of the group. This is especially important for the handicapped children since it focuses on aspects of their person that are normal rather than on the handicapping condition. Movement songs that use parts of the body that the handicapped child can move are also important to include, since this helps the child develop gross-motor skills and coordination. Finger plays are especially beneficial for orthopedically handicapped children who are having difficulty with fine-motor skills. In addition, songs can be selected that emphasize a particular speech sound that the orthopedically handicapped child is working on. If the orthopedically handicapped child is having problems with memory, the teacher should include some very repetitive songs, which are easier to remember.

Rhythmic activities are also important for the orthopedically handicapped child. These activities develop a rhythmic awareness, which may be lacking if the child's movements have been severely restricted. Clapping activities help develop rhythmic awareness and eye-hand coordination, and chanting emphasizes listening discrimination and speech skills. All these areas may be underdeveloped in the orthopedically handicapped child.

Movement activities may need more modification for the orthopedically handicapped child than do singing and rhythm activities, but they should not be eliminated since they are beneficial to both the normal children and the orthopedically handicapped child. The teacher should include some activities that use parts of the body that the orthopedically handicapped child can move so that he or she can participate fully. For example, if a child is crippled from the waist down, the teacher can plan swaying activities or movements that emphasize arm motions. For movements that the orthopedically handicapped child cannot execute, other methods of participation can be devised. The child might wish to recreate the motions using hands and arms rather than the whole body. Another alternative is for the orthopedically handicapped child to perform the movements with a puppet. (The other children might want to try this, too.) The orthopedically handicapped child might also wish to accompany the movement activity by playing on a drum. If other children ask to use puppets or instruments, the teacher should encourage this since it makes the orthopedically handicapped child feel that his or her activities are important and desirable, and it makes everyone feel more a part of the group.

Playing instruments is a very valuable activity for orthopedically handicapped children since it helps them develop fine-motor skills, eye-hand coordination, listening skills, and concepts of sound. Some modification in the playing of instruments may be necessary for some orthopedically handicapped children. For example, bells can be tied to the wrist of a child who is unable to hold the bells.

Some children have the use of only one hand; others cannot coordinate their hands well enough to hold an instrument with one hand and play it with the other. These children can be helped by having triangles, cymbals, and tone blocks suspended from frames so that only one hand is needed to play the instrument. On an instrument such as the autoharp, these children can either strum or push the buttons if they cannot do both simultaneously. Maracas and bells can be played with one hand.

Some children have such poor coordination that they have difficulty hitting a drum with a mallet. It may be easier for these children to play the drum with their hand or elbow. The teacher can help orthopedically handicapped children with poor fine-motor coordination play the xylophone by removing all the bars not necessary for the accompaniment.

In other areas of the music program, such as listening activities and learning about musical concepts, the orthopedically handicapped child can participate along with the other children. If the orthopedically handicapped child has difficulty concentrating, an adult sitting close by can help focus attention and make sure the child is comfortable.

CHILDREN WITH LEARNING DISABILITIES

The term *learning disability* is used to cover a variety of problems associated with difficulties in understanding or in using language, both spoken and written.[7] Learning disorders include such conditions as perceptual handicaps, brain injury, minimal brain dysfunction,[8] dyslexia,[9] and developmental aphasia.[10] The following behaviors are associated with children with learning disabilities, but it is unlikely that any given child would exhibit all or even most of these characteristics.

- Impulsiveness.
- Distractibility.
- Short attention span.
- Inability to follow directions.
- Hyperactivity.
- Perseveration.[11]
- General awkwardness and uncoordinated movements.
- Handedness not established.
- Conflict with other children.
- Self-help problems.
- Visual-motor problems.
- Cognitive delay.
- Social problems.
- Difficulty with bilateral movement, crossing the midline, and cross-lateral movement.
- Balance problems.
- Problems with spatial orientation and visual perception.
- Poor fine-motor development.
- Speech problems.
- Problems with auditory discrimination and auditory memory.[12]

Music and Children with Learning Disabilities

The learning-disabled child can benefit from music activities in many ways. First of all, music groups can help the child learn to relate to others in a social setting and develop a better self-concept. If songs are included that utilize each child's name or allow each child to contribute to the song, the self-concepts of all the children are enhanced. This is especially important for learning-disabled children, who may have low self-esteem as a result of their difficulties in functioning in the environment. Music experiences can also make learning-disabled children feel part of the group.

Another area in which music activities help children with learning disabilities grow is language development. Singing songs, chanting, and following the directions in songs build vocabulary and encourage the development of expressive and receptive language. Some learning-disabled children have particular difficulty with prepositions.[13] Songs such as "Put Your Finger on Your Nose" (Example 2.17) emphasize prepositions and help the learning disabled child develop an understanding of them. The teacher can alter the words to include other prepositions such as *over, under, in front of, behind,* and *beside.*

> Put your finger on your nose . . .
> Put your finger behind your back . . .
> Put your finger over your head . . .
> Put your finger in front of your knee . . .
> Put your finger beside your hand . . .

Music activities also help the learning-disabled child develop auditory discrimination and auditory memory. Playing listening games, playing instruments, learning to recognize concepts such as *loud* and *soft* or *high* and *low*, and performing rhythms all help children develop auditory discrimination. Singing songs, clapping rhythms, and performing ostinati encourage the development of auditory memory.

Learning-disabled children with fine-motor problems and visual-motor problems can benefit from several music activities. Clapping and playing instruments help them in fine-motor development and also aid children with poor visual-motor integration in learning to make their hands follow signals from their eyes. Finger plays also help learning-disabled children develop fine-motor control.

Large-motor skills can also be improved in learning-disabled children through music activities. Balance and coordination are helped by movement activities; specific movements such as jumping, hopping, and skipping can help the child develop better body control. Some learning-disabled children have problems with bilateral movement, which involves moving both arms and hands at the same time.[14] The teacher can devise specific dramatic movements that encourage development in this area, such as pretending to lift heavy boxes, to dig with a large shovel, or to rock a baby with both arms. Another area in which some learning-disabled children have problems is cross-lateral movement, or using opposite arms and legs at the same time.[15] Crawling activities, such as pretending to walk like bears, can help children develop these skills. Another motor problem encountered by some learning-disabled children is crossing the midline of the body.[16] Such children may color the right side of the paper with the right hand and the left side of the paper with the left hand, or eat food on the right side of the plate with the right hand and food on the left side of the plate with the left hand. Playing the xylophone can help with this problem if children are encouraged to use only one hand. Children will need to cross the midline in order to play all the bars on the xylophone. Playing the autoharp can also help since children must cross the midline in order to strum properly. Some creative movements, such as pretending to paddle a canoe, also encourage children to cross the midline.

Yet another area in which music activities can help learning-disabled children is following directions. Movement songs with specific directions emphasize this. Children are also encouraged to follow directions when playing instruments in a particular way, such as loudly or softly. Maneuvering through the whole group experience requires the child to follow many directions, and the teacher can help the learning-disabled child by making these directions as simple and specific as possible.

Planning Music Activities for the Learning-Disabled Child

Each area of music helps learning-disabled children overcome particular problems. Singing helps them develop better language, auditory discrimination, and auditory memory, and also encourages them to follow directions. Rhythmic activities help learning-disabled children learn to move rhythmically rather than with jerky motions, and also help them develop listening skills. Learning-disabled children benefit in many ways from playing instruments. Sound concepts are developed; fine-motor control and eye-hand coordination are improved; and sound localization, a common problem in learning-disabled children, is improved. Movement activities can help alleviate the many gross-motor problems associated with learning disabilities. Because each area of music deals with specific problems common to learning-disabled children, it is especially important for the teacher to include music activities from all these areas.

Learning-disabled children may have specific problems in handling the group music situation, which the teacher should consider when planning. Since some learning-disabled children have problems with hyperactivity, pacing is especially important. Such children may become over-stimulated by prolonged movement activities, so quiet and active activities should be alternated. A relatively fast pace for the group, with primarily short activities, also helps learning-disabled children. In addition, alternating types of activities and including a wide variety of activities help learning-disabled children maintain attention.

Some learning-disabled children have trouble understanding complex language and following directions. For this reason, the teacher should include in the lesson some short, simple activities that are easy for learning-disabled children to understand. The teacher should also make certain that all directions are stated as simply and directly as possible, and that learning-disabled children are given only one direction at a time.

Some learning-disabled children have problems with spatial orientation—understanding their position in space in relation to the objects around them. Other children may have difficulty sharing space with other children. The teacher can help these children by providing each child in the group with his or her own mat to sit on. This helps define each child's space and is especially helpful to the learning-disabled child.

Transition time is a difficult part of the day for many young children, and this may be especially so for learning-disabled children. The teacher should prepare for transitions carefully. The children should be prepared in advance for the transition to music and should be told clearly what activity is coming next during the music period. The teacher may need to stay near learning-disabled children to help them handle the transition to and from music. Following a set routine from day to day is also helpful for children with learning disabilities.

Children are considered to be seriously emotionally disturbed when they are identified by a professionally qualified person (psychologist or psychiatrist) as requiring special services.[17] Children who are emotionally disturbed may demonstrate an inability to build and maintain satisfying interpersonal relationships. They may exhibit inappropriate or immature types of behavior or feelings under normal conditions, or may remain continually in a particular mood regardless of what happens. In addition, emotionally disturbed children may be any of the following:

- Overly aggressive toward others.
- Self-destructive.
- Severely withdrawn or noncommunicative.
- Hyperactive.
- Severely anxious or phobic.
- Depressed.
- Psychotic.
- Autistic.[18]

Additional characteristics associated with emotionally disturbed children include:

- Learning disabilities.
- Communicative disorders.
- Awkward movement (withdrawn children).
- Sedentariness (withdrawn children).
- Perseveration.
- Poor self-concept.
- Difficulty in identifying and expressing feelings.
- Problems with learning skills.
- Difficulty in asking for and accepting help.[19]

**Music and Children
with Emotional
Disturbances**

Music experiences are very beneficial to children with emotional problems. Music activities encourage withdrawn children to participate with the group; children who typically refuse to talk may join in the singing. Paradoxically, although music encourages the withdrawn child to be more active and communicative, it also has a calming effect on many overly active or aggressive children. Both groups seem to benefit equally from the experience if it is carefully planned and implemented.

Music is also important to emotionally disturbed children because it supplies a ready means for the release or expression of emotion. In addition, it provides a positive outlet for the energy of overly active children. Singing, playing instruments, and performing movements are all good outlets for releasing suppressed emotions in disturbed children, as well as positive outlets for energy.

Music activities can help emotionally disturbed children with motor development. Clapping rhythms, playing instruments, and creating movements all encourage the sedentary child to be more active. They also help the withdrawn child, who may exhibit awkward movements, to develop better coordination and more fluid movements. Hyperactive children often have trouble controlling their body movements. They seem to move their whole bodies much of the time. Carefully planned movement activities can help the hyperactive child isolate body movements and develop better coordination. For example, a song such as "Put Your Finger on Your Nose" (Example 2.17) requires the child to use just one hand to point to various body parts. "The Hokey Pokey" (Example 2.16) also isolates body parts and movements. Movements such as hopping on one foot, bending, and pretending to get dressed also concentrate on one part of the body at a time.

Some types of emotionally disturbed children, including those who are anxious, aggressive, and hyperactive, have problems with fine-motor control. Clapping rhythms, playing instruments, and doing finger plays encourage development in this area.

Many emotionally disturbed children have poor self-concepts. Successful music experiences can help children with poor self-esteem feel better about themselves. In addition, songs that include all the children's names, what they are wearing, what they did during the day, and so on encourage a positive self-concept in every child. This is particularly important for children with low self-esteem.

Planning Music Activities for the Emotionally Disturbed Child

Some special accommodations may have to be made if the emotionally disturbed child is to feel comfortable in the music group. First, the teacher should be especially careful to prepare disturbed children ahead of time for the transition to the music group. All children benefit from preparation for transitions, but this is especially important to children who are emotionally disturbed since they often have more difficulty handling changes than other children.

The teacher should give special consideration to seating arrangements for emotionally disturbed children in the group. An aggressive child should be seated near an adult who can help him or her maintain control. It also helps to seat an aggressive child between two nonaggressive children. Hyperactive children should be seated near an adult who can help them focus their attention and maintain concentration. An anxious child may feel more comfortable sitting away from other children but near the group, or next to a very calm child. Confused or distractible children need to be close to an adult who can help them attend.

It is helpful to disturbed children if the teacher follows a familiar sequence both during the day as a whole and during the music group. Structure makes the anxious child feel more secure and helps children who are confused, aggressive, or hyperactive maintain control. The teacher can add familiarity to the group situation by always starting with the same song, at least until the disturbed child feels very comfortable in the group situation. Following a familiar sequence of activities also helps the disturbed child, as does including many familiar activities. New instruments, noises, movements, and the like should be carefully explained ahead of time so that the disturbed child has plenty of time to prepare for the change.

Teachers should use simple words and directions when talking to disturbed children. Some emotionally disturbed children become confused easily, and others cannot attend long enough to benefit from long explanations. Some emotionally disturbed children may need to be shown the task and physically moved through it.

Careful organization of the music group is especially important for emotionally disturbed children. Many short activities should be planned for children who are hyperactive, confused, or aggressive since they often have difficulty attending to longer activities. Pacing of the lesson is particularly important since emotionally disturbed children quickly lose control in high-stimulus activities such as creative movement, and have trouble attending to a long series of quiet activities. Therefore, quiet activities such as singing and listening should be alternated with active activities such as movement or playing instruments. The group should end with a quiet, familiar song so that the children leave the group feeling calm and secure.

Maintaining control in the group situation is particularly difficult for some emotionally disturbed children. They need consistent limits and clear expectations in order to learn acceptable group behavior. The teacher should maintain an acceptable volume level since excessively high volume is disturbing to anxious children and often overstimulates hyperactive or aggressive children. Keeping emotionally disturbed children actively involved in the group by calling on them frequently and planning a variety of activities also helps emotionally disturbed children maintain concentration and control.

CHILDREN WITH HEARING IMPAIRMENTS

Children with hearing impairments are commonly classified as either hearing-impaired or deaf. Hearing-impaired children have slightly to severely defective hearing, as determined by their ability to use their remaining hearing in daily life. Hearing loss is between 26 and 92 decibels in the better ear. Deaf children have hearing that is so defective as to be essentially nonfunctional in daily life. Hearing loss is greater than 92 decibels in the better ear.[20] Most children, even those classified as deaf, have some residual or remaining hearing. The following characteristics may be present in hearing-impaired children:

- Reception of sounds not as loud.
- Reception of sounds with distortion.
- Difficulty in communicating.
- Social and emotional problems.
- Cognitive delay.
- Delay in language development.
- Speech problems.[21]

Music and Children with Hearing Impairments

Children with hearing impairments benefit greatly from music experiences. This may seem paradoxical at first, but it is important to remember that most hearing-impaired children, including those classified as deaf, do have some residual hearing. Many music activities enable the hearing-impaired child to use that residual hearing. Hearing-impaired children also use visual clues to help them experience music activities.

Music activities can help the hearing-impaired child develop a feel for rhythm, which is very important for speech development. By watching other children, hearing-impaired children can see rhythms that they cannot hear. They can also feel rhythms by clapping along with the group, playing instruments with the group, and performing rhythmical body movements.

Music activities can also help hearing-impaired children develop another important skill—sound discrimination. Playing instruments encourages this. Some instruments, such as the autoharp and melody instruments, have wide enough pitch ranges to ensure that most hearing-impaired children will hear at least some of the sounds. Good-quality, low-pitched drums can also be heard by many hearing-impaired children. Music activities may encourage hearing-impaired children to develop better listening skills and to notice sounds around them.

Music groups also provide a socializing experience for hearing-impaired children. Active participation and feeling part of the group increase their self-esteem. In addition, the music group provides many opportunities for peer modeling.

Planning Music Activities for the Hearing-Impaired Child

Special consideration should be given to the hearing-impaired child when planning music activities. For example, hearing-impaired children should sit close to the teacher so that they can hear as well as possible and also make maximum use of visual clues. Songs should be simple, with repeated sounds, since these are easier for the hearing-impaired child to understand.

Rhythm activities are very beneficial to children with hearing impairments. Rhythmic activities such as clapping and chanting help the hearing-impaired child gain a feel for rhythm, which is important for speech development. Children who cannot hear rhythms use visual clues to help them clap along with the group; this allows them to feel the beat with their bodies. Many hearing-impaired children can hear rhythms if they are played on a low-pitched, good-quality drum.

Movement activities also help hearing-impaired children develop a feel for rhythm. Children who do not hear rhythms use visual clues to help them perform the movements the other children are doing. Hearing-impaired children should also have an opportunity to perform free movements not related to sound or dependent on visual clues, so that they have an opportunity to experiment with moving their bodies in a variety of ways and creating their own movements.

Playing instruments is perhaps the most important music activity for hearing-impaired children. Through experimenting with instruments and feeling their vibrations, they learn to feel rhythm, hear and discriminate between sounds, and feel the pulse of the music. The autoharp is an excellent instrument for the hearing-impaired child. Its wide pitch range enables it to be heard by more children than an instrument with a narrow pitch range. The same is true of melody instruments such as good-quality xylophones and glockenspiels. Although the hearing-impaired child may not be able to hear all the tones, the wide pitch range ensures that some tones will probably be heard. Some hearing-impaired children can even learn to match pitches—to sing the same tones as they play on the xylophone; this is very beneficial to their speech development.

Drums, if they are relatively low-pitched and of good quality, are also good instruments to use with hearing-impaired children. Many hearing-impaired children can hear the sound of the drum, and they can also feel its vibrations.

Other percussion instruments that are good to use with hearing-impaired children are sand blocks, sticks, and maracas. Hearing-impaired children can feel the vibrations of the sand blocks as they pass over each other. Although they may not hear the clicks of the sticks, they can feel the vibrations as the sticks strike and learn to play them rhythmically. Maracas have tactile appeal and enable the children to feel the vibrations as they are shaken. Because the triangle is high in pitch, hearing-impaired children may be less likely to hear the sound. If other children are playing triangles, however, hearing-impaired children should also be encouraged to participate with the group. The teacher might wish to remove the triangle holder and have the hearing-impaired child hold the triangle in his or her hand in order to feel the vibrations.

The teacher would normally not physically assist children when performing rhythms, since as children develop they gradually acquire a feel for the beat and rhythm in music.

In the case of the hearing-impaired child, however, the teacher may wish to gently take the child's hands and help him or her clap the beat if visual clues alone do not seem to be enough. This would be done only periodically and for short periods of time. The teacher might choose to assist the hearing-impaired child in this way because developing a feel for rhythm is so important to the speech development of hearing-impaired children.

CHILDREN WITH MENTAL RETARDATION

Children who are mentally retarded exhibit significantly below-average intellectual functioning accompanied by impairment in adaptive behavior.[22] They may exhibit the following characteristics:

- Overall slowness in development.
- Slower rate of learning.
- Difficulty remembering what they have learned.
- Difficulty solving problems.
- Limited language.
- Less ability to do things independently.

Mentally retarded children are customarily divided into categories depending on their degree of retardation: mild, moderate, severe, and profound. The following characteristics are typical of children in these classifications.

Mild Mental Retardation

- Learn more slowly.
- May have trouble speaking.
- May have trouble remembering.
- May have difficulty following directions.
- Have problems with eye-hand coordination.
- Are slower to learn routines.
- Have limited language.
- Are less independent, need more help.
- Have problems with fine-motor skills.

Moderate Mental Retardation

- Motor development delayed, clumsy.
- Very late in talking.
- Trouble remembering things.
- Developmental age about half of chronological age.
- Limited language.

- Require help with all daily needs.
- May have special problems with movement and feeding.
- May never learn to speak.
- Usually also have physical or neurological handicaps.[23]

Most retarded children who are mainstreamed are either mildly or moderately retarded. Therefore, these are the children considered in this chapter.

Music activities can help mentally retarded children develop in many areas. First, concrete experiences with sound and music can further the cognitive development of the mentally retarded child. Singing and playing a variety of instruments help the child form important concepts about sound.

Music and Children with Mental Retardation

Music activities also help mentally retarded children learn to focus attention and develop concentration. Repeating familiar songs and activities helps them develop their memory capabilities.

Language development is also furthered by music activities. Songs with explicit directions increase the vocabulary of mentally retarded children. Music activities also help the children develop listening skills, and listening facilitates language development. In addition, music activities help retarded children learn to sequence thoughts. Activities such as pretending to get dressed to go outside follow a sequence; if the teacher verbalizes this sequence in simple terms, mentally retarded children can begin to form sequencing concepts. For example, the teacher might say the following as the children act out the motions:

> First we put on our warm coats.
> Then we zip our coats.
> Next we put our hats on.
> Now we put our boots on.
> Next we put on our mittens.
> Now we're ready to go outside.

Some songs, such as "Put on Our Socks" (Example 9.1), emphasize a short sequence. This song is appropriate for mentally retarded children because it is short and easy to understand.

Example 9.1
PUT ON OUR SOCKS

Sally Moomaw

Put on our socks, Put on our shoes,

Then we can go out to play.

Motor development is another area in which mentally re-tarded children benefit from music activities. Many moder-ately retarded children tend to be sedentary, and movement activities encourage them to use their bodies. Specific move-ments such as hopping, galloping, and jumping help develop large-muscle control, as do creative movements. Fine-motor control and eye-hand coordination are developed through clapping, playing instruments, and finger plays.

Music experiences also help mentally retarded children develop socialization skills, and participating with the group builds self-esteem. In addition, songs and rhythms that in-clude each specific child's name build positive self-concepts in all children.

Planning Music Activities for Mentally Retarded Children

When conducting music activities, the teacher should give careful consideration to the language used with mentally retarded children; simple, direct language and one-step direc-tions should be used since mentally retarded children have difficulty understanding more complex speech. The teacher may need to show the mentally retarded child directly how to clap, play instruments, perform movements, and so on if the child does not understand the verbal directions.

Mentally retarded children benefit from having their sit-ting space clearly delineated in group situations. Having a mat for each child is one way to define each child's space clearly. It is also helpful to have another adult sit near the mentally retarded child to repeat directions if necessary, show the child how to perform activities, or help focus attention.

Teachers should give careful attention to the mentally retarded child when planning the content of the music group. Short, simple activities are desirable. Since a moderately retarded child of four will have a mental age of about two, activities on the toddler level are more appropriate than are activities for older preschoolers. The songs and activities should contain familiar subject matter that can be understood by the mentally retarded child as well as the other children. Retarded children are better able to remember activities that are repeated over a long period of time.

Finally, the teacher should give special attention to the mentally retarded child during transitions to and from the music group. Transitions are confusing for many children, and this may be particularly true with mentally retarded children. The teacher should give simple instructions to mentally retarded children; if necessary, the teacher or another adult can walk through the transition with them.

CHILDREN WITH VISUAL IMPAIRMENTS

Children with visual impairments include those who are both partially sighted and blind. Children who are partially sighted have central acuity of less than 20-70, with corrective lenses, in either eye. This means the child can identify an object in the direct line of vision at 20 feet that a normally sighted child can identify at 70 feet. A child is also considered partially sighted if peripheral vision is limited to an angle of 140 degrees or less or if other loss of visual function restricts the learning process. Children who are blind have such limited vision that they must rely on hearing or touch as their primary means of learning; have central acuity that does not exceed 20-200 in the better eye, with corrective lenses; or have peripheral vision limited to an angle of 20 degrees or less. The majority of blind children have some remaining vision.[24] Children with visual impairments may exhibit any of the following characteristics:

- Mannerisms such as rocking the body, fluttering the fingers in front of their face, nonstop tapping, and the like.
- Unresponsiveness.

- Developmental delay.
- Problems with large- and fine-motor development.
- Delay in learning self-help skills.
- Highly developed verbal skills, memory, and listening skills.
- Balance problems.[25]

Music and Children with Visual Impairments

Music activities can help visually impaired children develop important skills in many areas. Listening skills are a good example. Although visually impaired children may already show good development in this area, it is crucial that they continue to develop the ability to hear, listen carefully, and make close sound differentiations to the fullest extent of their ability since impairment of vision will force greater reliance on aural perception. Playing instruments, listening carefully for sound differentiations, listening to and performing rhythms, listening to words in songs, and following the directions of songs can all help visually impaired children maximize the development of aural skills.

Music can also help visually impaired children develop fine-motor skills. These skills are often underdeveloped in visually impaired children because visual clues are typically relied on for normal development in this area. Playing instruments, clapping, and performing finger plays can help visually impaired children develop better fine-motor skills.

Gross-motor skills are improved through music activities. Some visually impaired children tend to be sedentary, and music activities such as playing instruments, moving to music, and clapping encourage them to be more active. Movement activities can also help visually impaired children develop better balance, better localization of their bodies in space, improved coordination, and increased ability to localize body parts. In addition, the teacher can use music experiences to help visually impaired children learn specific skills such as hopping.

Music activities help visually impaired children as well as other children develop language and speech skills. Singing, performing rhythms, listening, and creating specific movements help children develop memory, concentration, vocabulary, and the ability to follow directions.

Music also gives visually impaired children an opportunity to develop socialization skills. Many music activities, by their nature, allow the visually impaired child to be immediately successful. Singing, hearing sound differentiations, reproducing rhythms, and playing instruments are all areas in which visually impaired children may excel. Being successful participants in the group can help visually impaired children develop positive self-concepts.

Planning Music Activities for the Visually Impaired Child

Special consideration should be given to the needs of visually impaired children when planning music activities. These children should be seated close to the teacher so that they can make maximum use of their residual vision. It is helpful if a second adult is seated near each visually impaired child to assist the child when necessary in learning movements, following directions, or playing an instrument. It is also helpful to visually impaired children if their own physical space and that of the other children is delineated by individual mats. The teacher should make certain that the lighting is appropriate for the visually impaired child. Many visually impaired children need relatively bright lighting in order to maximize use of their residual vision; others may have eyes that are sensitive to the light, and may see better and feel more comfortable in more subdued lighting.

When exploring music with visually impaired children, the teacher should discuss the music, instruments, and so on in terms of characteristics that the child can understand. The teacher can emphasize the sounds produced, the way the instrument feels, its weight and size, and the like.

Visually impaired children benefit greatly from experiences with instruments. They should be encouraged to explore a variety of instruments tactilely and to listen carefully to the sounds produced. In some cases they may need to be shown physically how to hold and play an instrument since they cannot rely on visual clues to learn this. Visually impaired children can learn to accompany songs on the autoharp by memorizing the chords. For children who read braille or will be learning to do so, braille tabs can be placed on the autoharp buttons. Playing drums may be easier for visually impaired children if they first use one hand rather than a mallet. Playing instruments that require coordination between two hands, such as sticks, triangles, or tone blocks, may be difficult at first for the visually impaired child. It may help if an adult helps the child hold the instrument still while the child plays it. Maracas and bells are very easy for the visually impaired child to play without help.

Visually impaired children may initially be fearful of performing movements. The teacher can start by introducing stationary movements such as bending or swaying so that the child can remain in one spot while performing the movement. Gradually other movements can be introduced that require the child to move about in space. These initial ambulatory motions might include crawling or rolling, since these keep the child in contact with the ground. The visually impaired child may need to be shown physically how to hop, gallop, or perform the movements in songs, since children usually learn these movements through visual clues.

The teacher should be certain to prepare visually impaired children for transitions. This is important for all children, but it is especially necessary for visually impaired children who may not be able to observe the teacher's preparations for the next activity.

CHILDREN WITH SPEECH OR LANGUAGE IMPAIRMENTS

Children are considered speech- or language-impaired when their problem with speech or language is serious enough to affect their self-concepts, their ability to learn, or their ability to get along with others. Speech and language disorders include receptive and expressive language impairment; stuttering; chronic voice disorders; serious articulation problems; and speech and language problems accompanying conditions of hearing loss, cleft palate, cerebral palsy, mental retardation, emotional disturbance, multiple handicapping conditions, and other sensory and health impairments.[26] In addition to their speech or language problems, these children may have difficulty with socialization and poor self-concepts.

Music and Children with Speech and Language Impairments

Music activities have special value for children with speech and language impairments. Music activities help language-impaired children in several ways. First, they encourage the children to focus their attention and to develop concentration. Also, many activities, from singing to acting out the movements in songs with directions, help the language-impaired child develop imitation skills. Music activities encourage development of language comprehension, sequencing skills, and vocabulary. In addition, the teacher can select songs that encourage the children to develop more complex language structures.

Children with articulation problems also benefit from music experiences. Many of these children have problems with auditory discrimination; music activities such as producing and listening to sounds, playing and identifying instruments, and listening for particular aspects of music help them develop better auditory skills. For children with articulation problems, the teacher can select songs that emphasize the sound or sounds they are working on. "How Does It Go?" (Example 9.2) has verses that focus on many of the difficult sounds for children with articulation problems.

Music activities also help children who stutter. Singing is an excellent activity for such children since most stutterers do not stutter when they sing. Repeating words and phrases in unison, as in many rhythmic activities, also helps stutterers, as does reciting well-known material such as familiar chants. In addition, music activities can help stutterers, as

Example 9.2
HOW DOES IT GO?

TAPE
(1st & 3rd verses)

Sally Moomaw

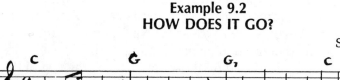

How does the snake go? s   s   s   s   s   s   s   s.

How does the snake go? s   s   s   s   s   s   s   s.

   2. How does the car sound when it won't start? k, k, k, k, k.
   3. How does the monkey go? Chee, chee, chee.
   4. How do the children sing? La, la, la.
   5. How does the baby go? d, d, d.
   6. How does the race car go? Brum, brum, brum.

175

well as other children with speech and language impairments, develop better listening skills, better socialization skills, and more positive self-concepts.

Planning Music Activities for the Speech- and Language-Impaired Child

Few modifications are necessary for speech- or language-impaired children to participate in music activities. It is helpful if these children are seated relatively close to the teacher so that they can hear and see well. Some speech- or language-impaired children may not be accustomed to sharing space with other children. Individual mats can help each child define his or her own space. In addition, the teacher should be careful to use clear, simple directions when talking to children with receptive language problems.

MAINSTREAMING EXCEPTIONAL CHILDREN IN MUSIC ACTIVITIES

Music is an excellent socializing experience for both handicapped and nonhandicapped children. In addition, both groups derive many benefits from music experiences. The challenge for the teacher is to plan successful music experiences that meet the needs of both handicapped and nonhandicapped children. Children with handicaps such as visual impairment, speech impairment, or orthopedic impairment can perform many activities at the same developmental level as nonhandicapped children, so mainstreaming these children into group music experiences is not difficult. Other children, however, such as those who are mentally retarded or emotionally disturbed, may need activities that are substantially shorter or simpler than those required by the rest of the class. In this situation the teacher must rely on compromise, creativity, and ingenuity. The teacher can alternate simple activities with more complex activities and thus meet the needs of both groups. The teacher can also select longer activities that have characteristics the handicapped child can relate to, such as songs with a repeated refrain. The handicapped child may not understand all the verses but can join in on the refrain. Creative movement activities allow some children to perform elaborate, complex movements while others perform simple movements. Orff activities also allow for a wide range of developmental differences, since less advanced children can perform simple ostinati while older children perform more complex patterns. Finally, the teacher may decide that some children should participate in only part of the group experience rather than for the entire group time. In that case the teacher can plan the simpler activities for the beginning of the group and the more complex activities for later on when the handicapped child may be working in another part of the room.

SUMMARY

Music experiences are important to the development of exceptional children just as they are to the other children in the class. Each type of exceptionality derives special benefit from certain aspects of music. When planning music activities for exceptional children, the teacher should set goals based on how music can help in the development of the exceptional child as well as the other children. Certain modifications in the environment or in planning may be necessary if the exceptional child is to derive maximum benefit from the music experience.

NOTES

1. U.S. Senate, Subcommittee on Education of the Committee on Labor and Public Welfare, *Education of the Gifted and Talented* (Washington, D.C.: U.S. Government Printing Office, 1972), p.10.

2. Appreciation is expressed to Dawn Denno for sharing this information.

3. *Spina bifida* is a congenital condition in which one or more of the bones in the spine fail to close. An opening is thus created in the spinal column.

4. *Cerebral palsy* is a disorder resulting from brain damage that affects posture, muscle tone, and movement.

5. For more information, see U.S. Department of Health, Education, and Welfare (Office of Human Development Services), *Mainstreaming Preschoolers: Children with Orthopedic Handicaps*, by Shari Stokes Kieran, Frances Partridge Connor, Caren Saaz von Hippel, and Linda Gaines Hailey. Publication No. 78-31114 (Washington, D.C.: U.S. Government Printing Office, 1978), Chap. 4 and 5.

6. Ibid., p. 98.

7. U.S. Department of Health, Education, and Welfare (Office of Human Development Services), *Mainstreaming Preschoolers: Children with Learning Disabilities*, by Alice H. Hayden, Robert K. Smith, Caren Saaz von Hippel, and Sandra A. Baer. Publica-

tion No. 78-31117 (Washington, D.C.: U.S. Government Printing Office, 1978), p. 11.

8. *Minimal brain dysfunction* is a delay or disorder in the ability to perform sensory or motor functions appropriately. See ibid., p. 10.

9. *Dyslexia* is the "impairment of the ability to read, or to understand what one reads silently or aloud, independent of any speech defect." Horace B. English and Ava Champney English, *A Comprehensive Dictionary of Psychological and Psychoanalytical Terms* (New York: David McKay, 1965).

10. *Developmental aphasia* is an impairment in the ability to understand and use spoken and written language that usually results from brain or central nervous system problems.

11. *Perseveration* is the continuing or repeating of an activity again and again.

12. U.S. Department of Health, Education, and Welfare (Office of Human Development Services), *Mainstreaming Preschoolers: Children with Learning Disabilities*, by Alice H. Hayden et al. Publication No. 78-31117 (Washington, D.C.: U.S. Government Printing Office, 1978), pp. 14, 35–39.

13. Ibid., p. 35.

14. Ibid., p. 35.

15. Ibid., p. 35.

16. Ibid., p. 35.

17. U.S. Department of Health, Education, and Welfare (Office of Human Development Services), *Mainstreaming Preschoolers: Children with Emotional Disturbance*, by Miriam G. Lasher, Isle Mattick, Frances J. Perkins, Caren Saaz von Hippel, and Linda Gaines Hailey. Publication No. 78-31115 (Washington, D.C.: U.S. Government Printing Office, 1978), p. 33.

18. Ibid., p. 33.

19. See ibid., p. 36 and Chap. 5 for more information.

20. U.S. Department of Health, Education, and Welfare (Office of Human Development Services), *Mainstreaming Preschoolers: Children with Hearing Impairment*, by Rita Ann LaPorta, Donald Ivan McGee, Audrey Simmons-Martin, Eleanor Vorce, Caren Saaz von Hippel, and John Donovan. Publication No. 78-31116 (Washington, D.C.: U.S. Government Printing Office, 1978), pp. 10–11.

21. Ibid., p. 10, Chap. 3.

22. U.S. Department of Health, Education, and Welfare (Office of Human Development Services), *Mainstreaming Preschoolers: Children with Mental Retardation*, by Eleanor Whiteside Lynch, Betty Howald Simms, Caren Saaz von Hippel, and Jo Shuchat. Publication No. 78-31110 (Washington, D.C.: U.S. Government Printing Office, 1978), p. 11.

23. Ibid., pp. 12–13.

24. U.S. Department of Health, Education, and Welfare (Office of Human Development Services), *Mainstreaming Preschoolers: Children with Visual Handicaps* by Lou Alonso, Pauline M. Moor, Sherry Raynor, Caren Saaz von Hippel, and Sandra Baer. Publication No. 78-31112 (Washington, D.C.: U.S. Government Printing Office, 1978), pp. 12–13.

25. Ibid., Chap. 2.

26. U.S. Department of Health, Education, and Welfare (Office of Human Development Services), *Mainstreaming Preschoolers: Children with Speech and Language Impairments*, by Jacqueline Liebergott, Aaron Favors, Caren Saaz von Hippel, and Harriet Liftman Needleman. Publication No. 78-31113 (Washington, D.C.: U.S. Government Printing Office, 1978), p. 13.

SELECTED BIBLIOGRAPHY

Alvin, Juliette. *Music for the Handicapped Child*, 2nd ed. London: Oxford University Press, 1976.

Cole, Frances. *Music for Children with Special Needs*. North Hollywood, Calif.: Bowmar Records, 1965.

Coleman, Jack L., et al. *Music for Exceptional Children*. Evanston, Ill.: Summy-Birchard Company, 1964.

Gallagher, James J. *Teaching the Gifted Child*, 2nd ed. Boston: Allyn & Bacon, 1975.

Graham, Richard M., and Beer, Alice S. *Teaching Music to the Exceptional Child*. Englewood Cliffs, N.J.: Prentice-Hall, 1980.

U.S. Department of Health, Education, and Welfare (Office of Human Development Services). *Mainstreaming Preschoolers: Children with Orthopedic Handicaps*, by Shari Stokes Kieran et al. Publication No. 78-31114. Washington, D.C.: U.S. Government Printing Office, 1978.

U.S. Department of Health, Education, and Welfare (Office of Human Development Services). *Mainstreaming Preschoolers: Children with Learning Disabilities*, by Alice H. Hayden et al. Publication No. 78-31117. Washington, D.C.: U.S. Government Printing Office, 1978.

U.S. Department of Health, Education, and Welfare (Office of Human Development Services). *Mainstreaming Preschoolers: Children with Emotional Disturbance*, by Miriam G. Lasher et al. Publication No. 78-31115. Washington, D.C.: U.S. Government Printing Office, 1978.

U.S. Department of Health, Education, and Welfare (Office of Human Development Services). *Mainstreaming Preschoolers: Children with Hearing Impairment*, by Rita Ann LaPorta et al. Publication No. 78-31116. Washington, D.C.: U.S. Government Printing Office, 1978.

U.S. Department of Health, Education, and Welfare (Office of Human Development Services). *Mainstreaming Preschoolers: Children with Mental Retardation,* by Eleanor Whiteside Lynch et al. Publication No. 78-31110. Washington, D.C.: U.S. Government Printing Office, 1978.

U.S. Department of Health, Education, and Welfare (Office of Human Development Services). *Mainstreaming Preschoolers: Children with Visual Handicaps,* by Lou Alonso, et al. Publication No. 78-31112. Washington, D.C.: U.S. Government Printing Office, 1978.

U.S. Department of Health, Education, and Welfare, (Office of Human Development Services). *Mainstreaming Preschoolers: Children with Speech and Language Impairments,* by Jacqueline Liebergott et al. Publication No. 78-31113. Washington, D.C.: U.S. Government Printing Office, 1978.

10
Planning for Music Groups

CHAPTERS 2 through 8 deal with the many areas of music that can be valuable in the development of young children. Each aspect of music—songs, rhythm, instruments, movement, listening, musical concepts, and Orff ideas—should be explored by the teacher and children throughout the day. Group music experiences for interested children are also valuable. Many aspects of music, from clapping rhythms to accompanying songs with rhythm instruments, can be covered more comprehensively in a planned group experience. In addition, music groups can provide a situation in which children can make the social change from isolated or small group experiences to participation in larger groups, if they are permitted to decide when they will join the group.

Careful planning must precede any successful group experience. Beginning the group, planning the content of the material, pacing the group, and ending the group must be given careful consideration. Longitudinal planning is also important.

The music group should begin with an activity that is familiar to the children. Beginning with a familiar activity encourages **BEGINNING THE GROUP** immediate participation and gives the children time to settle into the group before new activities, which require more focused attention, are started. It is generally best to begin with a familiar song since singing tends to calm the children and helps them make the transition to the group activity. More active parts of the lesson, such as movement or playing instruments, can be saved for later in the lesson when the children have adjusted to being with the group.

PLANNING THE CONTENT OF THE MUSIC GROUP

Careful consideration must be given to all the individual activities that will take place in the music group. The number and type of activities to be included and the relationship of the activities to the rest of the curriculum are important.

Number of Activities

The number of activities that can be included in a group experience will depend on the age of the children, the time of the year, and the children's previous experiences. In general, younger children need shorter group experiences than older children, because they cannot concentrate for as long. A group for toddlers might last for only five minutes; but since the individual activities would also be very brief, four or five activities could probably be planned for the five-minute period. Later in the year the toddlers might participate in groups for up to ten minutes. A group of three- and four-year-olds might start out with ten-minute periods and later expand to fifteen minutes. Five- and six-year-olds might begin with periods of from fifteen to twenty minutes and gradually work up to periods of twenty-five to thirty minutes; seven- and eight-year-olds might be able to handle thirty-minute groups from the beginning. Paradoxically, the number of activities per group may remain at around five to seven because older children can concentrate on individual activities of longer duration just as they can handle longer group situations.

Children who have had previous group experiences can often concentrate for longer periods of time in groups than can children who are having their first group experiences. Also, the concentration spans of individual children within the group will vary widely. The teacher needs to plan for those children who lose interest before the rest of the group. Perhaps another area of the classroom could be open for them, or an assistant or parent might sit by them in the group and help them maintain concentration by encouraging or modeling participation in the group activity.

Types of Activities to Include

Ideally, each music group should include at least one activity from each area of music—songs, rhythm, instruments, movement, listening, and musical concepts. In this way the children benefit from the areas of development that are particularly associated with each aspect of music. Covering each area of music is not nearly as formidable as it may sound. For example, if children accompany a song on wood blocks, they cover three areas—singing, rhythm, and playing instruments—in a single activity. Similarly, if children march to loud music and tiptoe to soft music, the three remaining areas—movement, listening, and musical concepts—have been included. The various areas of music are all so interrelated that planning inclusively for them all is not difficult.

It is also important to relate the music activities to the rest of the curriculum whenever possible. This reinforces concepts that are being studied in the classroom and makes the children familiar with the subject matter of music activities. For example, if the class is studying fall, the children can sing songs about autumn, chant and clap words associated with fall, and recreate through their movements falling leaves and nuts.

PACING THE LESSON

Part of the group planning should include the order in which the activities will be presented, so that pacing will be appropriate. Pacing is very important for maintaining the attention of the group and avoiding management problems.

When planning the sequence of activities in the group, it is important to alternate quiet and active activities. This keeps the children from becoming overly stimulated and helps them maintain concentration. Quiet activities include singing, clapping rhythms, chanting, and listening; more active activities include movement and playing instruments.

As stated earlier, it is best to begin the lesson with a familiar song. A quiet activity like this calms the children and invites early participation. After the opening song, a new activity that requires closer concentration can be introduced. This might entail learning a new song, clapping a new rhythm, or listening carefully for a particular aspect of music. Once this second activity has been completed, the children will have been sitting for a relatively long period of time, so a movement activity would be appropriate as a third activity. Something quiet should be planned to follow this more stimulating activity—perhaps another song or a listening activity. This might be followed by another more active activity, such as playing instruments. Such alternation of quiet and active activities keeps the children from growing restless from too much sitting or becoming overstimulated from too much moving.

Effective teaching techniques are also helpful in pacing the group. The teacher should begin quickly, without waiting for absolute silence, since the children's attention is quickly drawn once the song begins. The teacher needs to allow time for children's comments without becoming involved in long discussions that make the other children restless. Effective voice and facial expressions are also essential in maintaining group concentration.

ENDING THE LESSON

The lesson should end as it began, with a quiet, familiar song. Ending with a quiet activity helps the children settle down and compose themselves before making the transition to a new activity. Singing a familiar song enables everyone to participate in the closing of the group.

Many teachers like to end their music group with a transition song. Such a song enables the teacher to call the children's names individually and thus move children singly or a few at a time to the new activity, rather than all at once. The need for a transition song may depend on where the music group falls in the daily schedule. A song such as "Do You Know" (Example 10.1), to the tune of "The Muffin Man," is a good transition song because the teacher can add each child's name to the song along with what the child is wearing.

LONGITUDINAL PLANNING

In addition to planning for the beginning and ending of the group, the content of the lesson, and the pacing of the group, teachers also need to consider long-range planning for concepts that are developed over a period of time. Most music activities will become progressively longer, more challeng-

Example 10.1
DO YOU KNOW

Adapted from
"The Muffin Man"

Do you know   Er- in,   Er- in,   Er- in,

Do you know   Er- in, she has her blue dress on to- day.

ing, and more complex during the year; the teacher needs to sequence these changes carefully so that they follow a natural progression from simple to more difficult. Such longitudinal planning ensures successful learning experiences for the children.

Singing progresses gradually during the year from short songs with simple words to longer and more complex songs with more intricate melodies. Rhythmic activities also move from simple to complex, beginning with the chanting and clapping of single words and progressing to longer and more difficult chants, and perhaps to echoing. The introduction of instruments should also be carefully sequenced so that the children learn the sound of each individual instrument before the next is presented. Musical concepts are presented in a prescribed sequence, as presented in Chapter 7, so that the children build on previously developed skills as they approach more difficult concepts.

It is impossible and wholly undesirable for the teacher to plan a year's sequence of music activities at the beginning of the year. Such planning would disregard the children's interest and input as well as the rate of development of the class. Careful longitudinal planning involves planning a week or two at a time but always allows for spontaneity and input from the children to alter the plan. The teacher needs to keep in mind what the children have done in the past, what the immediate goals are, and how progress is unfolding toward meeting long-range goals. In addition, planning a week or two at a time allows the teacher to coordinate the content of the music activities carefully with the rest of the curriculum.

The following examples are provided to give some concrete suggestions for how group music experiences can be organized. The dynamics of each individual class will affect the actual plan developed by the teacher. These plans are presented as guides that can be added to or altered to meet the needs of each individual group of children. A diagram of each lesson is given, as well as the actual activities.

Two-Year-Olds Since this plan is intended for two-year-olds, who generally have short attention spans and limited language, the activities

Table 10.1 Sample Lesson Plan for Two-Year-Olds

Area	Activity	Why Selected
1. song	"Where is Jeffrey?"	Very short. Melody easy to sing. Each child's name can be added to the song.
2. rhythm, Orff	Clap names.	Simple beginning rhythm activity. Uses children's own names.
3. instruments, song	"Hear Our Jingle Bells" Children accompany song with jingle bells.	Short song with simple melody and words. Jingle bells easy to play and fit the words of the song.
4. listening, musical concepts	Listen and label loud and soft on drum.	Easy distinction to make between two sounds.
5. movement	"Step and Clap" Children follow directions in song.	Short, simple song. Directions easy to follow. Movements easy for two-year-olds.
6. final song	"Two Shoes"	Easy to sing for young children. Short, with simple words. Subject matter appropriate for two-year-olds.

are short and simple to understand. The activities deal with subject matter familiar to young children (see Table 10.1).

The name of each child in the group can be added to the song "Where Is Jeffrey?" (Example 10.2).

Activity 1

The child's first name can be clapped several times (see Example 10.3)

Activity 2

The children can accompany "Hear Our Jingle Bells" (Example 4.2) with jingle bells. Each child will need his or her own instrument. With older children, the activity would begin with everyone singing the song and clapping the beats. Two-year-olds, however, may have difficulty waiting that long for the instruments, so the bells are passed out at the beginning of the activity.

Activity 3

The teacher plays loudly and softly on the drum and labels each sound appropriately. The children listen for loud and soft sounds. The drum is used so that the children do not confuse pitch with dynamics.

Activity 4

For this activity, the teacher sings "Step and Clap" (Example 5.7) and follows the movements of the song along with the children.

Activity 5

The final song, "Two Shoes" (Example 10.4), is short and easy for all the children to sing. It can be sung several times.

Activity 6

Example 10.2
WHERE IS JEFFREY?

Where   is   Jef- frey?

Example 10.3
Chant of children's names

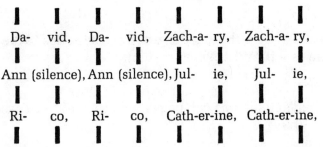

Da- vid, Da- vid, Zach-a- ry, Zach-a- ry,

Ann (silence), Ann (silence), Jul- ie, Jul- ie,

Ri- co, Ri- co, Cath-er-ine, Cath-er-ine,

Mar-ga-ret, Mar-ga-ret, Sean (silence), Sean (silence).

TAPE

Example 10.4
TWO SHOES

Original key: G major   Edna Ruff

Two shoes, new shoes, how they shine,
Two shoes, new shoes, they are mine.

Source: Laura Bryant and Edna Ruff, *Still
More Sentence Songs* (Cincinnati: Willis
Music Company, 1945). Used by permission,
Willis Music Co., Inc.

Three-Year-Olds This lesson is intended for a group of three-year-old children interested in the winter weather. The songs and activities are somewhat longer and more complex than are those designed for two-year-olds (see Table 10.2).

Activity 1 "It Was Snow" (Example 2.14) should be familiar to the children, since it begins the group. The teacher and children can sing it together.

Activity 2 Before beginning this listening game, the teacher plays each instrument while the children listen. Then the children can close their eyes and listen for which instrument is being played.

Activity 3 The children begin this activity by singing "Snowflakes" (Example 2.19) with the teacher. They can add new verses to the song as they discuss what snowflakes look like as they fall. Then the children can dramatize the actions of the snowflakes as the teacher sings the song.

The children begin this activity by singing "Jingle Bells" (Example 10.5) and clapping on the beat. Then the teacher distributes the bells, which the children use to accompany the song. If there are not enough bells for each child, the song can be repeated several times until each child has had an opportunity to play the bells.

Activity 4

Everyone can begin by singing the first verse of "We're Going to Build a Snowman" (Example 10.6). Then the children can add new verses as they decide what they would like to do outside. This song can be used as a transition song by adding each child's name to the beginning of the song.

Activity 5

Table 10.2 Sample Lesson Plan for Three-Year-Olds

Area	Activity	Why Selected
1. song	"It Was Snow"	Appropriate length for three-year-olds. Melody easy to sing. Coordinates with other areas of curriculum.
2. listening	Listening game: Compare triangle, bells, and wood block.	Encourages discriminative listening and aural memory.
3. movement, song	"Snowflakes" Children act out the motions of the snowflakes.	Encourages creative movement. Coordinates with curriculum. Encourages imagination as children add new verses to the song. Repetitive words and melody.
4. rhythm instruments, song	"Jingle Bells" Children sing the song and then accompany with bells on the beat.	Develops feel for the beat. Instruments fit the words of the song.
5. song	"We're Going to Build a Snowman" Children add new verses for what they will do in the snow.	Encourages creativity as children add new words. Coordinates with curriculum.

Example 10.5
JINGLE BELLS

Traditional

Jin- gle bells, Jin- gle bells, Jin- gle all the way,

Oh, what fun it is to ride in a one horse o- pen sleigh,

Jin- gle bells, Jin- gle bells, Jin- gle all the way,

Oh, what fun it is to ride in a one horse o- pen sleigh.

TAPE
(1st verse only)

Example 10.6
WE'RE GOING TO BUILD A SNOWMAN

Tune of "Go In and Out the Windows"

Sally Moomaw

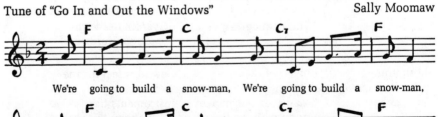

We're going to build a snow-man, We're going to build a snow-man,

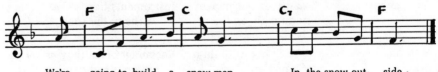

We're going to build a snow-man In the snow out- side.·

2. We're going to roll a snowball . . .
3. We're going to make it bigger . . .

190

The following lesson is planned for a group of four- and five-year-old children who are planning a trip to the zoo. Many of the activities are intended to help prepare the children for their trip. Since four- and five-year-olds generally have longer attention spans than three-year-olds do, and since the plan is for the end of the year, the individual activities and the total group period are longer than the one planned for three-year-olds (see Table 10.3).

Table 10.3 Sample Lesson Plan for Four- and Five-Year-Olds

Area	Activity	Why Selected
1. song	"The Elephant"	Coordinates with curriculum. Melody easy to sing. Clever words.
2. rhythm, Orff	Play names of zoo animals on tone blocks.	Coordinates with curriculum. Helps children divide words syllabically. Develops feel for rhythm.
3. movement	Act out zoo animals walking.	Encourages creativity. Develops gross-motor skills.
4. listening, musical concepts	"The Swan" Children listen for tempo.	Music depicts an animal the children will see at the zoo.
5. song	"The Hippopotamus"	Coordinates with curriculum. Interesting words.
6. listening	Sound effects tape, sounds of zoo animals.	Encourages careful listening. Prepares children for zoo trip.
7. song	"We Are Going to the Zoo" Children add new verses.	Coordinates with curriculum. Encourages creativity.

Activity 1   The children can sing "The Elephant" (Example 10.7). The opening activity should be a song that the children already know.

Activity 2   The children can think of zoo animals and then play the rhythm of each animal's name on the wood blocks. Each word should be played several times to give the children a chance to hear and feel the rhythm (see Example 10.8)

Activity 3   For this activity the children can select zoo animals and dramatize how they walk.

Activity 4   The children can begin this activity by looking at pictures of swans and talking about the animal. They can listen to the record (from Saint-Saëns's *Carnival of the Animals*) to hear

TAPE

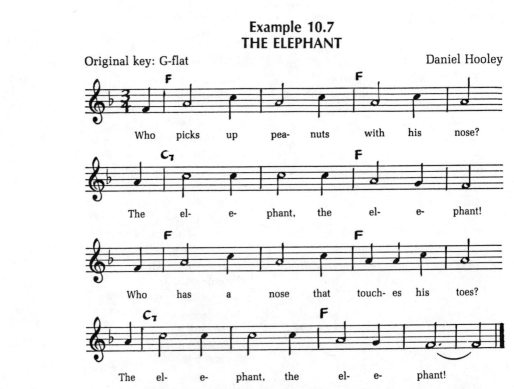

Example 10.7
THE ELEPHANT

Original key: G-flat

Daniel Hooley

Who picks up pea- nuts with his nose?

The el- e- phant, the el- e- phant!

Who has a nose that touch- es his toes?

The el- e- phant, the el- e- phant!

Source: From *Sharing Music*, Level K of the MUSIC FOR YOUNG AMERICANS series by Richard Berg et al., Copyright ©1966 (Cincinnati: American Book Company). Reprinted by permission of American Book Company.

192

how the composer uses music to represent the swan's movement.

The teacher can sing "The Hippopotamus" (Example 2.20) several times until the children know it well enough to join in. Then the children can act out the words of the song.

Activity 5

For this activity the teacher might select a sound effects record that includes the sounds of zoo animals, or tape record the sounds at the zoo. The children can listen to the recording or tape and try to identify the animals. Later, when they go to the zoo, they can listen for these same sounds.

Activity 6

The children can sing "We Are Going to the Zoo" (Example 10.9) to the familiar tune of "London Bridge." They can add many different animals to the song. The teacher can use this as a transition song by adding each child's name to the song in place of the word *we*.

Activity 7

Example 10.8
Chant of animal names

TAPE

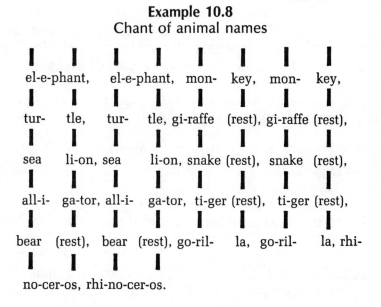

el-e-phant, el-e-phant, mon- key, mon- key,

tur- tle, tur- tle, gi-raffe (rest), gi-raffe (rest),

sea li-on, sea li-on, snake (rest), snake (rest),

all-i- ga-tor, all-i- ga-tor, ti-ger (rest), ti-ger (rest),

bear (rest), bear (rest), go-ril- la, go-ril- la, rhi-

no-cer-os, rhi-no-cer-os.

193

Example 10.9
WE ARE GOING TO THE ZOO

Tune of "London Bridge"　　　　　　　　　　　　　　　Sally Moomaw

We are go- ing　　to the zoo,　to the zoo,　to the zoo.

We are go- ing　　to the zoo　to　see the　an- i- mals.

Copyright ©1980 by Sally Coup Moomaw.

Six-Year-Olds This lesson is designed for a group of six-year-olds during the gloomy, rainy days of March. This plan contains more complex activities than do the previous ones, in keeping with the six-year-olds' growing maturity (see Table 10.4).

Activity 1 "Rain, Snow, and Hail" (Example 4.3) should already be familiar to the children since it is used to begin the group. After the children have sung the song, a child can accompany the singing with a simple ostinato on the xylophone (Example 10.10).

Activity 2 The children begin this activity by clapping three rhythmic patterns: "drip drop," "pitter patter," and "splash." Then the teacher divides the children into three groups and gives each group one type of instrument. Group I practices playing "drip drop" on wood blocks. Then group II plays "pitter patter" on triangles. Finally, group III plays "splash" on cymbals. Next the three groups are combined. Group I starts, then group II joins in, and finally group III is added (see Example 10.11).

Activity 3 The children skip when they hear the teacher play a long-short long-short pattern on the drum │$^6_8$ ♩ ♪ ♩ ♪ │ and march when they hear a steady beat.

Activity 4 The children can listen to this recording to hear how the composer uses music to depict a storm.

Activity 5 The children begin this activity by singing "Thunder" (Example 2.4) and clapping on the last three words of each line.

Next, several children play cymbals on those words while the other children sing the song. Finally, a child can add an ostinato on the xylophone. The song can be repeated several times so that everyone gets an opportunity to play an instrument (see Example 10.12).

The teacher can use "Rain, Rain, Go Away" (Example 8.8) as a transition song by adding each child's name to the song.

Activity 6

Table 10.4 Sample Lesson Plan for Six-Year-Olds

Area	*Activity*	*Why Selected*
1. song, Orff	"Rain, Snow, and Hail" Children sing the song and then one child accompanies the song on the xylophone.	Relevant to time of year. Appropriate song for Orff accompaniment.
2. rhythm instruments, Orff, listening	Children combine three different ostinati and play them on three percussion instruments.	Develops rhythmic awareness and listening discrimination.
3. movement, listening, rhythm	Children alternate skipping and marching to correspond to rhythms that teacher plays on the drum.	Coordinates movement with rhythm and listening skills.
4. listening, musical concepts	Storm section from Rossini's *William Tell Overture.* Children listen for dynamics.	Good example of tone painting by a composer.
5. song, instruments, Orff	"Thunder" Children sing the song and accompany with cymbals on certain words. One child plays an ostinato on the xylophone.	Relevant topic. Cymbals add tone painting. Encourages listening and rhythmic awareness.
6. transition, song	"Rain, Rain, Go Away" Teacher adds each child's name to the song.	Children can be called individually in the song to move to a new activity.

Example 10.10
RAIN, SNOW, AND HAIL

Sally Moomaw

Xylophone ▌ ▌ ▌ ▌

G   A   G   A

Can   you   hear the rain   etc.

TAPE

Example 10.11
Rain Sounds

Group I — Wood blocks   ▌ ▌ ▌ ▌

Group II — Triangles   Drip drop Drip drop

Group III — Cymbals   (wait for cue)

(wait)

Group I   ▌ ▌ ▌ ▌ ▌ ▌ ▌ ▌

Drip   drop   Drip   drop Drip   drop   Drip   drop

Group II   ⊓ ⊓ ⊓ ⊓ ⊓ ⊓ ⊓ ⊓

Pit-ter pat-ter Pit-ter pat-ter Pit-ter pat-ter Pit-ter pat-ter etc.

Group III   (wait for cue)   ▌   rest   ▌   rest

Splash   Splash

Example 10.12
THUNDER

Sally Moomaw

Xylophone ▌ ▌ ▌ ▌▌ ▌ ▌ ▌

G   A   G   A G   A   G   A

I looked up in the sky and saw a etc.

This plan for older primary children focuses on more complex rhythmic accompaniments than does the plan for six-year-olds. One of the songs is considerably longer than any used up to now. The Orff activities are also more complicated than are those used with six-year-olds. This plan uses late spring subject matter (see Table 10.5).

Seven- and Eight-Year-Olds

The children can sing "We're Going to Plant a Garden" (Example 2.6) together. Since this is the opening song, the children should already know it.

Activity 1

The children and teacher can say the chant "I Have a Garden" (Example 3.8), and then repeat it with a clapping, knee slapping, and stamping ostinato (Example 10.13).

Activity 2

Table 10.5 Sample Lesson Plan for Seven- and Eight-Year-Olds

Area	Activity	Why Selected
1. song	"We're Going to Plant a Garden"	Relevant subject matter. Length more challenging for older children.
2. rhythm, musical concepts, listening	Chant "I Have a Garden" with rhythmic ostinato.	Develops rhythm skills. Develops ability to separate fast and slow. Encourages sound discrimination. Relevant subject matter.
3. movement	Pretending to be clay.	Encourages creative body movements.
4. song, rhythm, listening	"Thunder" Accompanied by ostinati.	Develops ability to separate individual lines of music. Develops rhythmic skills. Encourages aural discrimination. Relevant subject matter.
5. listening	"The Cuckoo in the Woods"	Good example of tone painting in music. Relevant to final song.
6. song	"Bird Songs"	Closes lesson on a quiet note. Relevant subject matter.

Activity 3   The children can pretend to be clay, and the teacher can give suggestions for what is happening to the clay:

- Now the clay is rolled out smooth.
- The clay is rolled into a tube . . .
- . . . and then a ball.
- Now the clay is squeezed.
- The clay is rolled into a snake that gets longer and longer and thinner and thinner.
- The clay is pushed into a pile and left on the table.

Activity 4   The children begin by all singing "Thunder" (Example 2.4). Next three children compose ostinato patterns on a melody instrument. Then the song is begun, with first one ostinato starting, then the second, and then the third. When all three ostinati are playing together, the singing begins (Example 10.14).

Activity 5   The children listen to the recording and try to identify the sound of the cuckoo (from Saint-Saëns's *Carnival of the Animals*).

Activity 6   The lesson ends with the children singing a familiar song (Example 10.15).

SUMMARY   Careful planning of group music activities is essential in providing successful learning experiences for children. When planning the music group, the teacher needs to consider many things. First, the teacher must plan the content of the group. It is important to include activities from each area of music—singing, rhythm, instruments, movement, listening, and musical concepts—since each area focuses on a different aspect of music and develops different skills. The material should involve actual participation and experimentation in the music-making process by the children, since this is how they develop a real understanding of sound and music. In addition, the music activities should be coordinated with the rest of the curriculum so that the material is relevant and contributes to the total classroom experience.

    The teacher also needs to consider how to begin and end the music group, as well as how to pace the material. Beginning with a familiar song helps quiet the group and focus the children's attention, and it gives everyone a chance to participate immediately. The sequence of activities should be planned so that quiet activities such as singing and listening alternate with active ones such as movement and playing instruments. In this way the children do not become restless from sitting too long or overstimulated from too much movement. It is best to end with a quiet activity so that the

Example 10.13
I HAVE A GARDEN

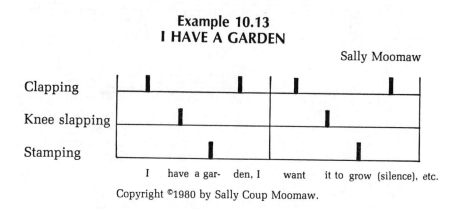

Sally Moomaw

Example 10.14
THUNDER

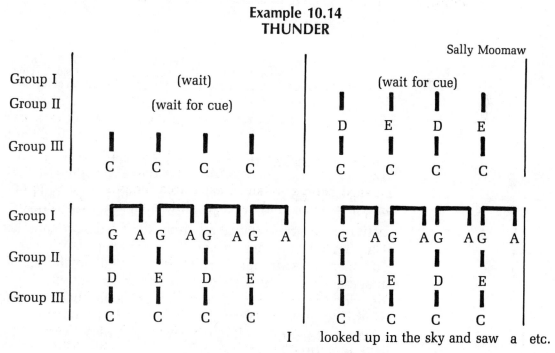

Sally Moomaw

Example 10.15
BIRD SONGS

Original key: E-flat

Katherine Davis

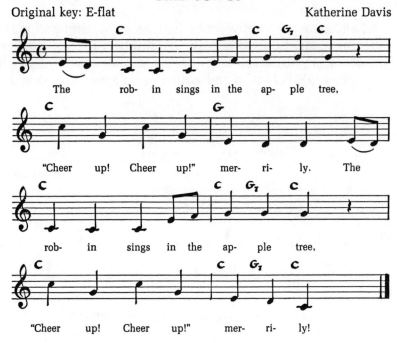

The rob- in sings in the ap- ple tree,

"Cheer up! Cheer up!" mer- ri- ly. The

rob- in sings in the ap- ple tree,

"Cheer up! Cheer up!" mer- ri- ly!

2. The cuckoo sings when the day is fair,
   "Cuckoo! Cuckoo!" ev'rywhere.

3. The great owl sings at the end of day,
   "Whoo! Whoo!" far away.

children can calm down before making the transition to a new activity.

In addition to considering the content and pacing of the group, the teacher should also plan longitudinally so that the activities progress sequentially from simple to more complex. Children develop musical abilities just as they develop skills in other areas, through active involvement in the music-making process and through performing activities that develop their skills sequentially. It is the teacher's responsibility to plan the music curriculum so that each child can develop him- or herself musically to the fullest extent of his or her abilities.

Glossary

Note: Any word marked with an asterisk (*) appears in this glossary.

accelerando (ack-CHEL-ler-AHN-doe): becoming gradually faster.

adagio (a-DAH-zhee-oh): very slow.

allegro (uh-LAY-grow): fast.

alto (AL-toe): low-sounding female voice (higher than tenor*) or medium-high-sounding instrument.

andante (ahn-DAHN-tay): slow—literally, at a walking pace.

bass (BASE): low-sounding male voice or instrument.

beat: steady recurrence of accented sound.

chant (noun): poem with a marked rhythmical character.

chant (verb): recite a poem or group of words in an accented manner so that a pulse* is apparent.

chord (CORD): two or more notes (usually three or four) sounding simultaneously.

choreograph (COR-ee-oh-GRAF): create specific movements to accompany music.

classical music: in pure sense, refers to music of the late eighteenth century. Used in common parlance to refer to music in the European tradition.

crescendo (cruh-SHEN-doe): becoming gradually louder.

decelerando (day-chel-ler-AHN-doe): becoming gradually slower.

decrescendo (DAY-cruh-SHEN-doe): becoming gradually softer.

dynamics (die-NAM-icks): degree of volume—that is, loudness or softness.

echo clap: an activity in which one person claps a rhythm* and another person or group of people clap the same pattern back.

forte (FOR-tay): loud.

glissando (glih-SAHN-doe): a gradual sliding up or down of pitch*.

glockenspiel: a percussion* instrument resembling a xylophone but having metal rather than wooden bars.

half-step: the interval* found between a white key on the piano and the black key adjacent to it, or between two white keys that do not have a black key in between (for example, E to F, or B to C).

harpsichord: an instrument with a keyboard like that of a piano, but whose mechanism plucks the strings inside rather than hitting them with hammers.

interval: distance in pitch* between two notes*.

largo (LAR-go): very slow.

major scale: a scale* in which the notes* follow the pattern, from bottom to top, 1 1 ½ 1 1 1 ½, where 1 is a whole step* and ½ is a half-step*.

mallet: a beater that one uses to strike a percussion* instrument.

melody: a succession of tones that forms a meaningful musical unit.

mezzo (MET-zo): medium. Mezzo forte is moderately loud, mezzo piano is moderately soft.

microtonal (my-crow-TOE-nal): music based on scales* whose formulas involve intervals* of less than a half-step*.

minor scale: a scale* in which the third note* is a half-step* lower than in a major scale*.

moderato (mah-dur-AH-toe): moderate speed.

nonpitched: refers to a percussion* instrument that does not sound a definite pitch* when struck or scraped. Examples are triangles, wood blocks, jingle bells, guiros, most drums, and so on. A xylophone, on the other hand, is *pitched*.

note: musical symbol that indicates the pitch* and duration of a musical sound.

ostinato (AHS-tih-NAH-toe): repeated pattern.

pentatonic scale: a five-note scale* in which the notes follow the pattern 1 1 1½ 1 1½, where 1 is a whole step* and 1½ is one and a half steps.

percussion: type of instrument whose sound is produced by striking or scraping.

piano (pea-AH-no): as an indication of dynamics*, soft.

pick: small template used by some guitar and autoharp players to strum the strings.

pitch: the degree of highness or lowness of a sound, which results from its number of vibrations per second.

polyphony (po-LIH-foe-nee): two or more melodies* played simultaneously.

presto: very fast.

pulse: same as beat*.

range: how high and low something (such as a song, an instrument, or a voice) goes.

resonant: resounding or reechoing. If, for example, a percussion* instrument is resonant, it will continue to sound for a few seconds after it is struck. The longer it sounds, the more resonant it is. If it is not resonant, it will produce a dull thud when struck.

rhythm: patterns of sound durations.

ritardando: (rih-tar-DAHN-doe): becoming gradually slower.

scale: a series of ascending notes* arranged to a prescribed formula of whole steps* and half-steps*.

skip: an interval* of more than a whole step*.

soprano: high-sounding female voice or instrument.

staff: musical symbol consisting of five lines on which notes* are placed. The note's position on the staff indicates its pitch*.

tempo: speed of the music.

tenor: high-sounding male voice (lower than alto*) or medium-low-sounding instrument.

theme: prominent musical phrase.

timbre (TAM-burr): tone color.

tone painting: use of music to depict a specific mood, event, scene, character, and so on.

whole step: interval* between two white keys on the piano that have a black key between them.

Index

Box, hollow, 78
Brahms, Johannes, *Hungarian Dance #5*, 121
Brake drums, 73–74
Britten, Benjamin, *A Young Person's Guide to the Orchestra*, 107
"Building Blocks," 19, 22

Carrot Seed, The (Ruth Krauss), 96, 102
Castanets, 56
Cerebral palsy, 154, 177
Chanting
  age levels and, 46–49
  and rhythm, 44–46
Chant of animal names, 193
Chant of children's names, 188
Characters, dramatizing, 88
Chords, 69
Clapping, rhythm and, 41–43
Classical music, 101–102
  movement to, 91–92
  records, 107–108
Claves, 54, 58, 59
Clock coils, 77, 78
"Clouds," 19, 21
Coconut shells, 70
Cognition, music for development of, 1–2
Concepts, musical, 9, 115
  dynamics, 115–120
  pitch, 124–129
  tempo, 120–124
Connor, Frances Partridge, 177
Copland, Aaron, *Billy the Kid*, 108
Cowbells, 58
Creative movement, *see* Movement
Crescendo, 118, 120
Cross-lateral movement, problems with, 158, 160
Cymbals, 55, 62, 63, 157, 194, 195
  finger, 56, 63

Dance, age level and, 97–99
Debussy, Claude, *Nocturnes*, 91
Decelerando, 121–122, 124

Decrescendo, 118, 120
Denno, Dawn, 102, 177
Developmental aphasia, 150, 178
Developmental stages, exploring music and, 4–7
Disks, pottery, 80, 81
Dog bark, 80
Donovan, John, 178
Doray, Maya, 102
Dowel harp, 73, 74
"Do You Know the Muffin Man?," 98–99, 184, 185
Dramatizing, dramatic movement, 94–95
  action, 88–90
  age levels and, 96
  characters, 88
  mood, 91
  to specific rhythms, 95–96
  stories, 96
Drums, 9, 43, 57, 59, 61, 63, 83, 84, 157, 173, 186, 187, 194
  brake, 73–74
  dynamics and, 116, 117, 120
  Latin American, 57
  log, 79
  Middle Eastern, 80
  Orff-type, 57
  snare, 57
  tempo and, 121–122
Drum talking, 50
Dvořák, Anton, *Carnival Overture*, 108
Dynamics, 115, 186
  age levels and, 119–120
  and crescendo and decrescendo, 118
  factors affecting, 117–118
  learning about, 116–117
  musical terms for, 120
  throughout the day, 118–119
Dyslexia, 158, 178

Echo clap, 49
Echoing
  age levels and, 50–51
  and rhythm, 49–50
Echo songs, 27–29, 49

About the Author

Sally Moomaw is an early childhood teacher at the Arlitt Child Development Center of the University of Cincinnati. She teaches a multiethnic class that includes Head Start children, non–Head Start children, and special-needs children and serves as a cooperating teacher for teachers in training. At the University of Cincinnati, she received a bachelor's degree in elementary music education from the College–Conservatory of Music and a master's degree in child development from the College of Education. She has given numerous workshops concerning music with young children and teaches a course on the subject at the University of Cincinnati.